A Promise Kept
The Life and Work of
Tom Chapman

Tom Chapman in the 1960s

A Promise Kept

The Life and Work of Tom Chapman

by

JOHN STEWART

SHEPHEARD-WALWYN (PUBLISHERS) LTD

© John Stewart 2003

All rights reserved. No part of this book may be
reproduced in any form without the written permission
of the publisher, Shepheard-Walwyn (Publishers) Ltd

First published in 2003 by
Shepheard-Walwyn (Publishers) Ltd
Suite 604, The Chandlery
50 Westminster Bridge Road
London SE1 7QY

British Library Cataloguing in Publication Data
A catalogue record of this book
is available from the British Library

ISBN 0 85683 218 9

Typeset by Alacrity,
Banwell Castle, Weston-super-Mare
Printed in Great Britain by Bookcraft (CPI Group),
Midsomer Norton

To Pat

Contents

Acknowledgements ix
Foreword xi
Introduction xiii

1 Devotion 1
2 Bleak Conditions 3
3 Twelve Young Men 7
4 Respect 12
5 Knowledge of the Heart 15
6 The Sea 18
7 The Communist Threat 21
8 The Mantle of the Church 29
9 The Age of Strikes 36
10 The Pilkington Strike 1970 39
11 Rolls-Royce and Chrysler 46
12 The Bridgebuilders 50
13 Conferences 53
14 Two New Unions 59
15 Education 63
16 Europe 67
17 The Cumbria Grand 72
18 The Trip to Moscow 77
19 Unity 82
20 The Need Remains 84

Appendices 87
Notes 119
Index 127

List of Illustrations

Frontispeice

Tom Chapman in the 1960s

Between pages 48 and 49

1 Stressful times for Tom Chapman and his wife Pat, November 1958
2 Act of Dedication in Westminster Abbey following a conference on 'Responsibility in a World Adrift', June 1971
3 Awarded an MBE in 1976
4 Attending first AGM of Graphic and Creative Arts Association, November 1981
5 Visiting the Kremlin, April 1993
   Evening years: Tom and Pat
6 Portrait by Charles Hardaker
7 Tom's Vision, painting by Charles Hardaker

Acknowledgements

MY GRATEFUL THANKS to Joan Crammond for typing the MS, including the innumerable additions and changes, and for her helpful editorial suggestions; to Pat Chapman for her willing co-operation and kindness when I visited Stainton; to Robert and Verena Watson, whose substantial input was vital; to the Revd Basil Watson, Patron of the ECIM, for his friendly welcome and willingness to be of assistance; and to the ECIM Trustees, James Armstrong, Peter Green, Iain Cairncross and Ian Mason for their substantial support; my thanks to Roger Pincham for his considerable contribution and to Richard Elias for relating his 'on the ground' experiences during the strike-bound era; to Jean Desebrock for her careful and detailed refinements to the text and to Anthony Werner, my publisher, for his guidance, editorial skill and patience.

I am grateful for David Pilkington's considerable help with the Pilkington chapter, and for Matt McGrath's warm-hearted co-operation. I am also very grateful to Timothy Glazier for his substantial support, indeed to all those who contributed and are mentioned in the text; to Carol Duncan, who passed on vital biographical notes, and to Claire Sack, now resident in Perth, Australia, who posted a weighty parcel of archive material, my sincere appreciation. My thanks to Claire Foster for her ready assistance with research and to Sergei Tarassenko whose contribution has so enriched the text. Thanks are also due to Bill Finley for his willing help with the chapter on the trip to Moscow, and Mark Pratt for his considerable contribution in recording Tom's recollections.

I appreciate Albert and Audrey Sandbank's help and take the opportunity to remember all the care and comradeship that the late Ron Heaps gave to Tom. It is obvious from the Europe chapter that the contributions of Joan Schoup, Hans Leewens, Luc and Leen Glorie, John Mansley and, of course, Verena Watson were essential. Very many thanks are due to them all.

I am indebted to both Neil Elles, who introduced me to the work of Common Cause, and Graham Pool, who responded so quickly; also to Hugh Lunghi, author of *The Common Cause Story*: the background information he provided was invaluable. I am also indebted to Ray Cross for his help.

My thanks to John Nelson of the Methodist Church for his help in providing biographic detail relating to the Revd William Gowland.

Acknowledgements are due to the following: Associated Newspapers for the use of the *Star* quotation dated 10th June 1958; the *Daily Mail* for the use of their text dated 4th November 1958; Express Newspapers for the substantial quotation from the *Daily Express* dated 3rd November 1958; Mirror Pix for the Cassandra column extracts from *The Daily Mirror*, 13th June 1958; the North Western Evening Mail for extracts from both the *Barrow News* and the *North Western Evening Mail*, September/December 1958; the Reader's Digest for the use of extracts from the September 1967 issue; and Times Newspapers Ltd for extracts from *The Times*, 12th November 1970, 6th February 1976 and 15th May 2002.

My thanks are also due to Penguin Books for permission to use an extract from *The Imitation of Christ* by Thomas à Kempis, and to A.M. Heath & Co Ltd for the passage from George Orwell's *The Road to Wigan Pier*, published by Penguin Books, 1962; and the quotation from A.J.P. Taylor's *English History 1914-45* is reprinted by permission of the Oxford University Press.

Foreword

THE LATE 1950s were a crucial time in this nation's history, with militant power poised to challenge and overthrow lawful government. The Communists, in their various groupings, encouraged and financed by the Soviet Union, were working with great resourcefulness and vigour to destroy the capitalist world – especially so in Britain. One of the most vulnerable areas for attack was trade unions, where a small but vociferous minority could have a disproportionately powerful influence.

The traditional labour leaders who wanted to reform, but not revolutionise, society found themselves being overwhelmed and replaced by militant communists, whilst the general membership remained apathetic.

For the average union member his loyalty to his union was sacrosanct but he wanted to be led without having to be involved in union politics. The democratic rules for electing the leadership were no safeguard when the silent majority did not excercise their votes. It was this desperately dangerous situation, coupled with the over-liberal approach of many 'progressive' intellectuals and journalists, that led to the founding of Common Cause, of which I was a Member of Council for many years. Although this abuse of union power did not succeed in bringing down lawful government, it is widely held that it destroyed the British motor industry. Common Cause was aware in 1957 that trade union leaders were concerned with the Communist stranglehold on certain areas of Britain's second largest union, the AEU. This was particularly true in the North London Area. Common Cause was also aware that these trade union leaders considered Tom Chapman the person who might win a forthcoming election in that area. Such an election took place and history relates that he beat the Communist candidate by one vote. Tom Chapman's fight against Communist aggression during his term of office is graphically described by John Stewart.

It was some months later that I first met Tom and became a member of his London Group. I attended several of his later conferences, including those at Scargill, near Kettlewell, and Grange-over-Sands in Cumbria, at which my wife Diana (Baroness Elles) became a frequent guest speaker. Tom took the view that he should not have been 'thrown in at the deep end' of union politics without proper training. I have no doubt that it was for this reason that he devoted much time and attention to detailed training in his groups and in teaching them the art of public speaking.

Tom was a very charismatic man who could mix easily in any company. He worked to dissolve dissension and to build bridges between the adversaries in any dispute. He was a committed Christian who believed that the power of love could conquer all evil and that it was his task to put this into practice. It is good that his story should be told, to remind us and future generations of how fragile is our hold on freedom and how dependent it is on good people speaking what they know to be true and acting as they know to be right and just.

NEIL ELLES, QC
Founder Member of Common Cause

Introduction

IN 1917 the Bolshevik revolution exploded on the streets of St Petersburg; it was a godless revolution which saw religion as 'the opiate of the people', the enemy that kept them quiet, acquiescent to tyranny.

The followers of Marx now had a tangible example of their master's theory. For seventy years a grotesque regime raped mother Russia, though at the time many altruistic converts in the West saw the revolution as a model holding the promise of a new Utopia – the hope of economic justice for the many who suffered from the harsh inequalities of the Victorian and Edwardian era. They did not see the iron hand of Soviet autocracy, a hand that reached beyond Russia's borders to control and dictate worldwide party policy.

With the benefit of hindsight we are amazed at those fashionable intellectuals who, it seemed, were taken in by carefully managed visits round showpiece Russian factories. The demonic enormity of the Gulag somehow was ignored. Did they not know about the harsh enforcement of collective farms and the resulting catastrophic failures of harvest? Perhaps it was excused as 'understandable'.

In 1941 Hitler launched 'Operation Barbarossa'; for Russia the 'Great Patriotic War' had begun. This titanic struggle between totalitarian giants cost many millions of lives,[1] but Russia triumphed with its Communist tyranny in place. The Party claimed the laurels; 'Uncle Joe' (as Stalin was perceived) was cheered in British cinemas. But the story did not end there. Communism, like a vigorous religion, gained new converts everywhere. Britain was no exception: there really were 'Reds under the beds', had we but known.

The trades union movement was a main focus of communist infiltration. Their brutal theory was simple: smash industry, bring the country to its knees and then take over. Some might say (as is often the case in Britain) that it was a near-run thing. This nation, with its freedom-loving ways, was vulnerable – yet we muddled through with our freedoms still intact.

Why did Communism fail in Britain? There were many reasons, but one is undeniable: it was a godless creed. The unions and Labour Party were influenced by Christian values. Before he entered the House of

Commons, the speeches of Philip Snowden, the prominent Labour Party member and lay preacher, were described as 'warming and idealistic', they 'helped materially make British socialism a gospel of love not hate'.[2] Moreover, this nation has a love of tolerance and fair play. Yet it was a battle: at the coalface the fight was very bitter. Men had to stand up and be counted. This was Tom Chapman's world.

The Berlin Wall, that monument to Communist failure, has been demolished but the battle is not over. The forces of disruption still abound, they just wear different clothes. If presently subdued, militancy is waiting in the wings.

*

In Tom Chapman's youth the poverty suffered by the general mass of working people was a breeding ground for communism, yet remarkably the Party failed to be a major force. They did not break the loyalty of the average worker to the Labour Party, his union and union leadership,[3] which were mainly Christian and royalist, with no wish for violent revolution. Lenin looked upon MacDonald and the Labour leadership as betrayers of the socialist cause. The British establishment, though they dreaded Labour's growing power, honoured the constitution and the sentiment of George V that 'they ought to be given a chance and ought to be treated fairly'.[4] Considering the savagery of the Russian revolution and the extreme language of some Labour supporters, the King's moderate tone was prudent, courageous and in the best British tradition. Not to have supported the moderate Labour leadership would have undermined them, opening the way for extremists.

It was after Labour's triumph in 1945, during those first post-war decades, that the militant threat grew serious. Russia, pumped up with her new world-power status, was forcefully spreading the Stalinist gospel. Ernest Bevin, Attlee's sensible Foreign Secretary, pointedly replied to the Russian Vyshinsky: 'I know when I displease the Soviet government because all the [trade union] shop stewards who are Communists send me resolutions in exactly the same language.'[5] Nye Bevan, who was considered to be on the far left of his party, used more colourful language: 'Communism is not a party but a conspiracy, a deathwatch beetle destroying our institutions from within.'[6]

The danger was all too real but, one suspects, not fully understood by the majority of the union membership, or the population at large, who were generally suspicious of conspiracy theories. So a group of influential lawyers and the like gathered to confront the danger. Freedom was their

'Common Cause' so this was the title they chose (see Appendix I). Their role was mostly educational: they used broadsheets, pamphlets, lectures and a mobile film unit to awaken sleeping Britain, but did not intervene directly in union affairs.

Common Cause was disbanded in 1994. Today their work does not receive an automatic reference in the history books, yet their efforts were a vital contribution to the preservation of the freedoms we too often take for granted.

Tom Chapman, a senior union leader, was well known to Common Cause. He was 'a great man', as one founder member emphasised. Tom was at the sharp end, eyeball to eyeball with the Communists, who tried every trick to break his will. It was a dirty business but Tom Chapman did not compromise his Christian principles: if he won the battle, he would claim it was the power of love which triumphed. How much the nation owes Tom Chapman and his like may never quite be known.

FRIENDSHIP

We have a great deal more kindness than is ever spoken. Maugre* all the selfishness that chills like east winds the world, the whole human family is bathed with an element of love like a fine ether. How many persons we meet in houses, whom we scarcely speak to, whom yet we honour, and who honour us! How many we see in the street, or sit with in church, whom, though silently, we warmly rejoice to be with! Read the language of these wandering eye-beams. The heart knoweth.

Ralph Waldo Emerson,
Essay on Friendship

* in spite of

CHAPTER 1

Devotion

A new commandment I give unto you, That ye love one another ...
St John 13:34

TOM CHAPMAN'S message was love, but it was a message communicated by his presence as much as by his words, and the manifestly obvious fact that he strove to practice what he preached. 'I have one qualification,' Tom said, 'one with which I speak with authority: the amazing power of love I know.'

He was no dewy-eyed do-gooder. Such hypocrisy he detested. If clever minds, put off by his constant theme of love, labelled him naive, they missed the mark. Tom's deep clear eyes were ever watchful: years of hard experience saw to that. He had no time for humbug. Tom's love was not possessive, for him it was God's love. It was inclusive and the commandment 'love your enemies' he struggled to obey. In disputes his first concern was to find a bridge that spanned the gap between parties. There was no time off. It was his constant work – God's work.

The power of faith in Christ and the all-embracing unity of Love are not mere concepts of the mind. Cerebral agility cannot conjure them up. They are as one, a grace by which needs are met with simple ease. Some call this knowledge of the heart, a sure and certain prompting to be voiced without fear of derision. In this Tom stood four square and firm.

Good employers rarely suffered strikes, Tom would maintain; it was where care was absent that strife walked in. Contemplating the ageless problem when only about twelve years old he precociously concluded that it was man himself who was to blame for strife and poverty – because he had forgotten God. It was 'a black and white situation', Tom recounted; 'with God remembered in the heart' how could greed and hatred rule? This early belief, matured by experience, never left him.

'I was ten when I started church as a choirboy,' Tom remembered. 'It happened by the grace of God. I know no other reason. My father was an ordinary decent working-class man who believed in God. The same went for mother, but they did not attempt to persuade me to accept their

1

beliefs. My belief was based entirely on what I had read in the Bible. In those days you did half an hour compulsory Bible study at school. People accepted it. Maybe they did it mechanically, but you could also do it with understanding.'

Tom was just short of his teens when he was confirmed. 'God', he emphasised, 'was a very close friend.' This sense of friendship was a constant source of strength throughout his life, and the well-spring of his love.

One sermon he recalled had a lasting impact. The text was 'Jesus wept' – just two words. He subsequently heard them many times, but the first time they carried power. Why had Jesus wept? The answer he received made a powerful impression: *People were not obeying his words.* To Tom this was an inescapable truth, the basis for a logical plan of action to set the world to rights. Looking back, he readily admitted his early naivety and presumptions, but the heart's intent remained, an enduring will to share God's love with all.

Tom was committed. On Sundays he went to church, first as a boy server, later as a Sunday school teacher; then to Bible class and, of course, to matins and evensong. He recounts how he talked to God every day and how the words 'Jesus wept' were ever in his mind.

In those days, that is the early thirties, there was stark poverty. It was about the worst time. I remember my father saying that this was how life was going to be unless we changed it. He meant politically, but I aimed to make people believe in God. This wasn't conceit. I genuinely did believe, for I was talking to God every day and he was the only one who was listening!

Tom was ordinary in that he naturally joined the rough and tumble of life – he was neither a fanatic nor a simpering 'holy Joe' – but he was extraordinary in that he openly followed the injunction: 'Man's chief end is to glorify God and enjoy Him forever.'

CHAPTER 2

Bleak Conditions

Wherever you are and wherever you turn, you will
not find happiness until you turn to God.
Thomas à Kempis, *The Imitation of Christ*[1]

THE LIVING conditions of the average working-class Briton between the wars, especially in the 1930s, were harsh. Families crowded into small cramped houses. A mother might buy food, but could she afford a bar of soap as well? Stark choices, and all too real when unemployment loomed.

When the call to strike arrived all knew the hardship it would bring. George Orwell, in *The Road to Wigan Pier*, paints a depressing picture:

As you walk through the industrial towns you lose yourself in labyrinths of little brick houses blackened by smoke, festering in planless chaos round miry alleys and little cindered yards where there are stinking dustbins and lines of grimy washing and half-ruinous WCs. The interiors of these houses are always very much the same, though the number of rooms varies between two and five. All have an almost exactly similar living room, ten or fifteen feet square, with an open kitchen range; in the larger ones there is a scullery as well, in the smaller ones the sink and copper are in the living room. At the back there is the yard, or part of a yard shared by a number of houses, just big enough for the dustbin and the WC. Not a single one has hot water laid on.[2]

*

Tom was born on 23rd October 1914 at 14 Duncan Street, Barrow-in-Furness, within easy walking distance of the Vickers shipyards. His father Henry is noted on Tom's birth certificate as a ship's packer. His mother's name was Agnes (née Dell). A good part of his childhood was spent in nearby Vincent Street. Speaking about conditions during his childhood, Tom painted a picture not dissimilar to George Orwell's though his family were more fortunate.

We were lucky in my house because my father had his own garden [probably an allotment], so we fed on what he produced. We also had pigs and these he was able to sell from time to time, so we were moderately well off and 'moderately', you have to realise, is no comparison to today.

3

Even when he was sixteen and earning the 'princely' sum of 5s 11d a week, Tom never had new shoes. They were 'always someone else's shoes'. So moderately was moderately.

We lived in a house with two bedrooms and an attic upstairs and two downstairs rooms with a kitchen, cold water. My father and mother had one bedroom to themselves, and then there were my three sisters who had the other bedroom. In the attic we had two brothers sleeping in one bed and three brothers sleeping in another... And we took it for granted this was what was happening in most ordinary houses.

Then there was bath night. How much we take for granted today.

There was one tub, for a bath. Bath night was on Friday. This was more or less regular throughout the various streets. In fact all the people I knew had a bath on Friday night. To get washed in cold water was, of course, the everyday occurrence. Those who did work used to get very dirty and to get the dirt off with cold water took considerable time and patience.

The Poor Laws, Tom pointed out, were grim: a visit from the Poor Law man could strip you of the few small treasures you might still have. It is not surprising that a hatred of the means test is entrenched in British culture. Then there was the dole, the consolation of the unemployed. It was, of course, minimal.

The Poor Law officer's job was to find out if you deserved the dole. He looked around your house and, if he saw something you didn't need, you'd be told to sell it, and if you didn't sell, no dole. This happened quite often. We were lucky. We had a piano and my father managed to persuade them this was desperately needed because he had several children who needed to learn the piano in order to get a job if possible later on. That's how we came to have the piano. I have to say that the Poor Law officer didn't know about the pigs! Neither did he know about the hens, and the fact that, because food in the house was reasonably cheap, we were able to live.

The Poor Law man also decided whether or not you could afford to pay the rent. If you couldn't afford to pay, you were evicted. This is where the homelessness came about. They had what they called the Cottage Homes which you could be taken to. We were very lucky and never were evicted, but I've seen evictions. They always took place on a Tuesday in those days. I've seen two or three piles of furniture outside a house. And you know, you couldn't find out what happened to the people. There was the workhouse, of course, and the Cottage Homes for children.

There was recourse to an appeal board, but it does not take a great deal of imagination to understand their nature: they were tough. Faced with an unremitting tide of woe, perhaps they felt that they had to be.

If you wanted to appeal against a sentence, or rather what this officer of the Poor Law had said, you had to appear before what was called the Board of Guardians. The father of the house, or the mother or whoever was available, had to appear and explain why they shouldn't be punished. Well, the people who were facing them were really hard. I remember one Councillor; I knew her son very well. She was a dreaded person to a lot of people. People wrote about the wonderful woman she was but I saw the lady. She was very rigid. If she thought that you were a scrounger or a sponger then, before you even opened your mouth, you were condemned. She was pretty typical of those on the Board of Guardians.

If you had no income at all and could not pay rent you could be put into the workhouse. I had two brothers who were over the age of sixteen. Now, if young men over the age of sixteen couldn't get a job, they were not allowed to sleep in their parents' house. They had to leave home and find jobs. That's why on Birkrick Moor, five miles away, they had bell tents where the people who couldn't stay in the houses used to sleep. The bright side is that boys like myself, ten years old and upwards, loved to spend almost the whole of the school holidays up on the Moor with our elder brothers, because it was a lovely, wonderful life, or so it appeared to us. We used to fill sacks with ferns, collect them and stick them together to sleep on. The dark side is that I was in hospital for probably just over ten months with what they called nephritis, a kind of pneumonia on the kidneys. I'm positive now that this was because the ferns were damp.

I enjoyed being in hospital. It was very lovely and refreshing. The nurses were wonderful and kind and the difference between now and then is terrific. The matron – you could hear her voice coming from well over a hundred yards away. She was the boss-dictator! Her heart was very kind, that must be clearly said, but she was a bully. The beds had to be very tidy; every window had to be wide open, always, in any weather. That was the matron's orders. The sisters and nurses were literally scared of her. But the patients didn't need to be. I was in hospital for so long that she became a great friend to me. I remember her to this day. When you reached her heart she was lovely. I used to assist the nurses making the beds. I became as expert as any of them, getting the corners of the sheets at 45-degree angles, absolutely correctly. The food in the hospital was very good. Others may disagree, but looking back over the years, it's as good, if not better, than it is today. I've been in hospital recently, two or three times over the past few years, the same hospital, same organisation as 60 years previously. The cleanliness is different. Some people may not like it, but I think it was cleaner in those early days than it is today. The nurses are as lovely as they were then! I've never met a nurse that I wasn't in love with![3]

*

Considering Tom Chapman's early experiences and the dark images described by George Orwell, it is little wonder that the creed of Lenin gained a following, the wonder is that it failed to triumph. Writing about the period of the general strike of 1926, A.J.P. Taylor observes:

The strikers asked for nothing for themselves. They did not seek to challenge the government, still less overthrow the constitution. They merely wanted the miners to have a living wage. Perhaps not even that. They were loyal to their unions and their leaders...[4]

Who were their leaders? Taylor comments that 'the general strike brought to the front the very men, such as [Ernest] Bevin and [J.H.] Thomas, who put conciliation before conflict.'[5] Why? Clearly the Communists in the Labour movement had failed to grasp the moment, though it was a classic moment for their stratagems. Labour was a growing force in Parliament and the Labour Party had briefly been in power in 1924. Extremism, distasteful to the British, would have frightened the electorate. Even so one needs to ask why the Labour movement was moderate despite the extremes of poverty that were the general lot of their supporters. Maybe Tom Chapman's schooling, with its daily half-hour of Bible reading holds the answer. If Tom's experience was common in those days, the poetry of the King James Bible must have had a lasting influence.

Today religious instruction is so circumscribed by legislation that the Bible-reading discipline seems remote. This is the age of the welfare state. Social democracy is espoused by all the major parties. Materially we are better off and most would say the bad old days are past, yet prisons are in crisis, overwhelmed by sheer numbers, drug abuse is rampant and violent street crime mounts. It would appear that, having reached the uplands of a better world, we have now lost our way. What has gone wrong?

Tom Chapman said that evil flourished where progress was 'unguided and defiant of God'. Jesus wept because the people had forgotten his words.

CHAPTER 3

Twelve Young Men

But be ye doers of the word, and not hearers only, deceiving your own selves.
For if any be a hearer of the word, and not a doer, he is like unto a man beholding his natural face in a glass:
For he beholdeth himself, and goeth his way, and straightway forgeteth what manner of man he was.
But whoso looketh into the perfect law of liberty, and continueth herein, he being not a forgetful hearer, but a doer of the work, this man should be blessed in his deed.
The General Epistle of James, 1:22-5

SOMETIME in the late twenties or early thirties, twelve young apprentices gathered inside the large cylinder of a condenser shell in the Vickers shipyard in Barrow-in-Furness. They were fitting plates and, as work was slack, they got to talking. Tom was one of their number. He did not record whether they had met by chance or by design.

They were all Sunday school teachers who shared a concern for the deprivation they saw about them, and with the energy of youth they set out to put it right! 'And it's still our ambition,' Tom maintained when in his eighties.

We all agreed that wrongs arose due to man's failure to accept God's laws. If only we could persuade people – I wince now at my conceit – if only I could persuade people to be as good as me. I didn't think it hypocritical, as I was really trying to be good, trying to be a Sunday School teacher and, looking around the group, each one of us seemed to be that kind of person. Why shouldn't we admit that we believed in God. All right, I've learnt a lot since then, but that's beside the point. The point is, we began this group to put the world aright with God's help. Then we split the world up, as it were, in that we all decided on the part that each of us should play.

To dismiss such youthful plans as wildly optimistic, arrogant and naive would be understandable, but such worldly-wise conclusions would be wrong. These young men were both serious and sincere: Tom's life is evidence of that. He continues:

It was an interesting group. As I've said, there were twelve of us, all roughly sixteen and upwards; eighteen was probably the oldest. The man that stands out in my mind most of all was the Managing Director's nephew, Craven. He was straight from University and going back to University after he'd done twelve months' apprenticeship. He was what we called a Premium Apprentice, which meant that his parents paid for his training. He was a very good man — the kind of Christian I've dreamt about. He treated us as equals and never put on airs. He was intelligent, but it was his kindness not to show it overmuch. Yet there was nothing at all patronising about his manner.

We agreed that he would become a Director, which he did and later, when in that position, he was able to help me many times; not only in Vickers but generally in my work as a Trade Union leader. His advice helped me considerably. As a Director, he never compromised his position by advising me how to fight Vickers but told me he would pray for us and look for right directions. That was his way. I always regarded him as a very close and wonderful colleague. I mean that, rather than just a friend, he was more than a friend.

The same goes for Arthur Hearsey. Two of the twelve had wanted to work for God as Members of Parliament. Arthur Hearsey got in through the Unions, while the other one never made it. It did not matter because he was very useful as a member of the Conservative Party.

Arthur's role was in the Labour Party. When he became a full-time Trade Union leader, we worked together very closely. He actually attended some of our conferences before he died. In fact he used to come to some of my early conferences where everybody was a trade unionist.

For Tom the Trades Union Movement was his chosen path. He joined the AEU (Amalgamated Engineering Union) and in his long career was never the tool of either militancy or management. Tom played it straight:

I joined the AEU not because I believed in Trade Unionism at the time, but because I believed that Christ would want me to join a living force that could do real work for the people and help them see the way God really works. I still think we were right because God works not only in our hearts but also in whatever we really try to do. I did try to be a good trade unionist and in my opinion I was.

Another member of the group became involved in the Co-operative Movement — a collection of organisations owned by and operated for the benefit of those using their services.[1] Tom explains:

Our role was to persuade whatever movement we were in that it was a piece of work for God and that there really was a brotherhood, a brotherhood of man. All of us held to our tasks and we met when we could. We agreed to meet at least once a year, to discuss what had happened and report. We stuck to it right until one by one death reduced our number. I'm the last one alive. We all kept our word.

Our objective became 'to turn the hearts and minds of men to God, that they may walk in His ways'. Now this is something all the organisations in which I've been involved have taken as their own. But it all began in that condenser shell and the man who eventually became a Director framed our aims, which we in turn developed.

There was the Church, of course; we all belonged to the church. Only two of us were Church of England. Arthur Hearsey, the Labour Member of Parliament, was a Methodist and three of us were Roman Catholics – very keen Catholics. We all had to recognise that the Church was solely concerned with what were called church activities, which did not include things such as the trade unions or the political parties. So our objective, on the advice of our friend Craven, whom I regarded as the leader of our group, was to keep the larger picture in mind.

What happened in that condenser shell in Barrow-in-Furness? Why did twelve young men commit themselves with such finality? True, they were Christians, Sunday school teachers, no doubt full of youthful vision at a time when the gospels were actually studied, yet there was something else. These young men were not merely aping custom; there was a depth of passion far beyond the surface gloss of piety.

In the early days this commitment may at times have been naive: it was ardour without direction, as Tom was ready to admit. He recalled how they preached to crowds at the corner of Duke Street and Abbey Road in Barrow while waiting for the dole. He remembered the ridicule as the twelve, one after the other, would speak, quoting from the Bible. They learned the hard way that there was no point in preaching to men 'picking up a few shillings to keep the family'. Talking about God's love in such a situation was a waste of time. The lesson was plain: 'by their works shall ye know them'; their attention needed to be directed to their various tasks.

Despite their different areas of work, the twelve met and shared their problems as often as they could. They debated questions like, 'How do you differentiate between a good Christian and a Socialist, or a Conservative, or a Liberal? Where do you find the difference?' The answer came much later: there was no substantial difference. As Tom said, 'A really true Socialist is as good as any true Conservative.' He always sought the common thread, the path of tolerance. Truth was the unifying factor, manifested through love.

One man who helped the twelve was a labourer who worked as a sweeper and odd job man in the condenser bay. Tom expands:

I discovered that he was a church warden at a parish church nearby. He was a wonderful man, not very clever, but it was he who taught me so much about what is good and what is bad in industry, and how to keep to your word. The words of wisdom that came from him! He was quite an old man; he must be dead at least forty years now, but I still remember his advice. I remember him telling me about smoking and girls and that I shouldn't listen to the way men talked abut women. It stuck in my mind. It didn't mean I was awfully good and all that, but what I avoided and what I still don't like are dirty jokes about women. 'Whatever you do,' he said, 'have nothing to do with such jokes.' I've always tried to stick to that advice.

He cared about the truth and how you spoke it. 'You know,' he said, 'you can tell your sister she's got an awful hat, but there's a nice way of saying it. You don't have to tell a lie, yet she'll realise the hat's not suiting her and she won't be hurt. So remember,' he said, 'the truth need never hurt anyone, if you tell it truthfully.' Well, that's one of the men that helped us stick together, the twelve that pledged their word, because we all admired and loved him.

The only clergyman involved with the group in those early days was the Revd R.W. Stannard, vicar of St James in Barrow, Tom's own parish church. Tom told this story:

The week before the Revd Stannard was called to our parish all those years ago, we had formed what was known as the Junior Church Council. This was open to those under 21 years of age and whatever was happening on the Parish Council we discussed at this level. We also had what they called a children's service. The children's service was at half past ten and the whole service was taken by the children, except for one thing – the blessing. When I took the service I dropped a real clanger. The Revd Stannard was there to take the blessing but I did it instead!

He remembered the sermon I gave long after I'd forgotten it and he came back to it time and time again. He would say, 'Do you remember when you said this?' Then he would repeat the statement, whatever it was.'

It seems that the Revd Stannard saw in Tom something special, the fire of sincerity perhaps, the fearlessness of conviction. Stannard later became Bishop of Woolwich and eventually Dean of Rochester. He was also Chaplain to the King from 1937 to 1941. Wherever he was called, Tom was invariably invited to preach or address meetings. He preached at Woolwich, at Rochester and at Fleet, where the good man, in his later years, was an honorary curate.

Tom's lifelong friendship with his old parish priest and mentor is a story in itself. They did not always see eye to eye. On one occasion Stannard attended a meeting of the group to protest about a strike they were supporting, but this did not dent the strength of their relationship.

He remained in contact with me and several other members of the group. Wherever I was, even when I went into the Merchant Navy, he would arrange for some clergyman or other to come and see me. Almost every time we set off on a voyage, there would be a knock on my cabin door and someone with a word from him would appear.

Our close relationship continued throughout my trade union activities and, when I became Advisor for Industry at Church House, he was on the Church Assembly as the Bishop of Woolwich.

Clearly Bishop Stannard was a major influence in Tom's life, a constant and supportive friend. The seeds of the friendship had been sown in Barrow – the same town in which twelve young men had met one day in a condenser shell and pledged their shared commitment.

CHAPTER 4

Respect

O! when degree is shak'd,
Which is the ladder to all high designs,
The enterprise is sick. How could communities,
Degrees in schools, and brotherhoods in cities ...
Prerogative of age, crowns, sceptres, laurels,
But by degree, stand in authentic place?
Take but degree away, untune that string,
And, hark! what discord follows.
                              Troilus and Cressida, I.3

WHEN TOM CHAPMAN was young the leaders of society expected and were shown respect. The boss was 'Sir' or 'Mister', never 'Bill' or 'Bob'. The old captains of industry were often paternalistic; they usually knew their workers by name and were not indifferent to their welfare. Sir Charles Craven, the uncle of Tom's friend, was one such man, and Tom looked up to him. Vickers, he always maintained, were good employers, but of course they worked within the customs of the time. Change was in the air though, dramatic change – some good, some not so good.

After the war working conditions substantially improved but Tom regretted the eroding of standards, especially of respect. Late in life watching a report on a Commonwealth Conference, he recalled: 'The Queen was present and when the national anthem was played no one stood up.' Tom was appalled: this was a corrosive example of visible disrespect. He preferred the days when a Bishop was called 'My Lord Bishop' rather than 'Bishop Bill' or 'Bishop Jack'. Though we may speak to Jesus Christ as a personal friend, those who represent him represent his awesome majesty. Bishops should not be afraid to speak with plain authority or stand against the degradation of social standards.

To call a teacher by his or her first name was quite simply wrong, Tom felt: where respect is scorned, anarchy prospers, as happens in too many of our classrooms. Such matters are often considered trivial, mere questions of fashion. Surely true respect is in the heart? Yet correct forms of address are marks of respect, reminders of what is due. Tom recalled:

At a public school that I go to for a lecture, probably four times a year, even when I walk into a room every boy stands up until I'm sitting down. That is respect to an older man. The respect due to a bishop should be even greater. A bishop could be a very young man but, because he's an ambassador for Christ, he must be recognised.

Tom was no right-wing misfit – nothing could be further from the truth. Rigidity was alien to his nature, but he always strove to honour people with respect. He took no one for granted. This was love in action.

*

Tom talked of the camaraderie between workers at Vickers. When Barrowians met abroad (something Tom experienced during his Merchant Navy days) the conversation always turned to marvelling at the great ships built at Barrow. In many ways Barrow was Vickers; when shipyard work was slack, Barrow suffered. 'We will build you anything from a pin to a battleship and from any kind of material.' Tom recalled Commander Craven's boast when desperate to gain work. They did diversify – making everything from tennis-ball moulds to cable gear for the goldmines in South Africa – and they renovated the Blackpool sewage system. 'Every kind of gun was made by Vickers.' Tom worked on 18-inch ones. He also had experience of almost every ship's engine that Vickers made.

As a schoolboy Tom was told that Vickers was the greatest engineering company in the world. 'We all believed it,' he remembered, 'and were proud to contribute.' This is Tom's description of a plater's team:

Four riveters were part of a plater's team. The noise in the plater's shop was deafening, so lip-reading became part of the job. One man would heat the rivets for the riveters. It is surprising how much skill was required to throw the red-hot rivet for the riveter to catch before it chilled and got too hard to fit. It was hard work but to my knowledge there was nobody who objected to it. Hard work was expected of a man and certainly I didn't feel any the worse for it.

Those were the days when the head foreman wore a bowler hat as a symbol of his status: respect was due and was shown. On the ladder of promotion one moved from cap to trilby and then to bowler. Respect for position and pride in craftsmanship were everyday virtues.

When Tom was an apprentice the only heating was from hot-air pipes. This had little effect on the factory floor, so drums peppered with holes were used as fire braziers. Tom recounts:

To stand round the fires and have a midnight snack on that shift is a pleasant memory. This was where older men would speak about their experiences and younger men would listen with anticipation. These tales were about men who could use their tools with greater skill than most. Pride in jobs was just as interesting as football is today.

CHAPTER 5

Knowledge of the Heart

What stronger breastplate than a heart untainted!
Thrice he is arm'd that hath his quarrel just,
And he but naked, though lock's up in steel,
Whose conscience with injustice is corrupted.
Henry VI Part 2, III.2.

As an apprentice fitter, Tom worked with a man called Bob Hornwell, an ardent member of the Plymouth Brethren. He preached wherever he went, for 'the Gospel was not only his creed but his everyday language. He was a wonderful man,' said Tom. 'He was big, well over six feet tall and he hardly ever lost his temper.' He always held on to his belief. His one failing, Tom recounted, was to entice *him* to his Gospel Hall with money for a visit to the pictures – a ploy known to most parents!

Because of his open commitment Bob Hornwell's leg was always being pulled and workmates jeered and catcalled him. The bullies loved this. At one stage Tom was working with him on condensers – very large tanks with tubes fitted and with doors at each end, an after and a forward door, which were of a completely new design. Tom continues the story:

I remember we had almost completed one, about a week's work, when suddenly he said, 'Tom, you know what I've done. I've put the forward end on the aft instead of the other way around.' Now I knew this was deadly serious and it would mean real trouble. I ran up to one of the men who had been jeering him and told him the whole story. At once he assembled all the others together and they started to work immediately their lunchtime began. They stripped the whole thing out with the crane driver helping. All of them worked for nothing, it was absolutely unofficial. The foreman was giving the instructions what to do. Every stud had to be replaced, because it was a different type of size, so it was literally a week's work. Twenty men worked as a team on various machines and within one hour they had the whole thing completely finished and put back. If ever there was a miracle that was it.

What is interesting, never once did any of them complain or mention that job, in all the years I knew them. They continued to jeer him and skit him but none of them ever mentioned the fact that he had done a job the wrong way round, for he would almost certainly have got the sack.

15

This 'miracle'. as Tom maintained, was to him a powerful confirmation that God was there in every heart.

At the beginning of the Falklands War, when transportation needs were desperate, a ship refit which was scheduled to take weeks was completed in little more than one weekend, the usual obstacles forgotten. When the heart responds to need, the shackles of the mind are blown away. Tom understood this.

By nature Tom was clear-sighted and decisive. He saw what was before him and, if necessary, he acted. There was no debate, no 'Should I?' or 'Shouldn't I?' What was more he had a kind of extra sense. Once, when leaving a country house where some friends met for study weeks, instead of driving as usual towards the main gate, he suddenly turned left towards the stables, obeying an impulse. Then he saw Paddy, who lived in the stables, lying face-down in a puddle. Tom turned him over and revived him; another minute and Paddy would have drowned. Could it be that such knowledge is given to those whose hearts are open?

On another occasion, when Tom was riding on the back platform of a bus, he saw a man abusing a woman. As the bus was slowing down in traffic Tom jumped off, gave the man a straight upper-cut, and leapt back on to the bus. It was all done in a flash. The reaction of a friend who was with him was, 'How can you square this with your Christian principles?' 'Ah,' replied Tom, 'I hit him in love!'

*

Tom's method of Bible study was to read a passage and then refer it to what God himself told him within his own heart. God was his constant guide – speaking through that still small voice. Tom was certainly not a fundamentalist, accepting every word in the Bible as holy writ. The Bible had been written and translated by men. The 'I'm right and you're wrong' rigidity of belief was not for him. He knew there was more than one road.

One might say, for example, 'That flower is very beautiful.' Someone else would refer to the same flower because of its colour or because of any of the diverse aspects of the word flower. What is accepted by all of us, whatever we may see, is that God produced the flower. That is what really matters.

We have in the mind's eye a vision of Jesus Christ but the inner man of Jesus Christ is the most profound – the perfect vision. I believe what it says: that He'll come again and we'll see once more that perfect picture.

Christ is in my heart – definitely! There is no such thing as accepting Him because He is already there. You may reject Him or you may welcome Him in His fullness. You cannot half accept Him; it must be full. How I wish my own acceptance of

Him might be full, but we cannot wish this for ourselves alone. Our task is all around us.

He used the Lord's Prayer as a guide through daily life but he was never 'holier than thou'. His efforts encountered powerful opposition: 'The devil fought me all the way and I met enemies from every conceivable direction,' yet he always remembered Christ's commandment, 'Love your enemies.' Tom saw this as his duty, '... and – do you know? – it's fascinating how I kept to this.'

CHAPTER 6
The Sea

Thou, O Lord, that stillest the raging of the sea, hear, hear us, and save us that we perish not.
The Book of Common Prayer

TOM CHAPMAN worked at Vickers in Barrow until his early twenties, when he was offered a job at sea. For one blessed with the vigour of youth this was an exciting opportunity: he accepted with alacrity. This was a year or so before the war.

Vickers provided a repair squad for ships in trouble and Tom was a specialist in oil: if anything went wrong with a ship's oil flow, he was the expert to hand. During his time in the Vickers engineering shop he had gained his first, second and third tickets, qualifying as a chief engineer, though he acted in this capacity only once, when the incumbent was taken ill. The repair squad wore uniforms, an officer's one for Tom, and of course lower ranks were obliged to salute – 'if they noticed you', Tom added knowingly. He was ill at ease with his new status. The uniform and all that went with it seemed unreal although he liked being on the open sea. 'I've been round the world five times at least,' he reminisced. He sailed with several P&O ships, the battleship *The Prince of Wales* and the liner *Strathmore* during the Spit Head Review (the passengers were foreign royalty and Tom met them all).

Before all this, while still an apprentice, Tom had occasionally been selected for submarine trials – 'a tremendous thrill'. That was Tom. His enthusiasm was infectious.

*

Tom was at sea when war broke out, still with the Vickers repair squad.

At first you did not realise the war had broken out except for the dimmed lights. To me it meant nothing until the first time we had a near miss. I was by the side of the ship with the chief engineer, looking out at sea. He was telling me what to look for: a trail of foam on the water – the tell-tale sign of a torpedo. I said to him: 'Like that one there?' The chief engineer screamed like blazes, 'Action stations!' The

18

boat swung round and the torpedo just missed us. It was quite a thrill. Had it not been for the chief engineer alerting me, we would not be talking here today. So many things happened – so many near misses. I was intended to live, no doubt whatsoever. For example, I was in a submarine when it was recalled to port. I was transferred to another ship and the submarine went to sea without me. It was never seen again. After that it happened twice that I was told to change from boats that later disappeared. Once I had appendicitis that stopped me going out.

So many times I have been called somewhere and as a result I am here today. Everybody has miracles like that in their life. Often people do not even notice them.

It did seem that Tom led a charmed life. One astonishing event he recounted only to his closest friends. Those who knew him well will remember two deep scars on the corners of his mouth. Were they a legacy of a clash with left-wing bullyboys, or an explosion on a torpedoed ship? Had the whiplash of a snapping hawser cut him? Though curious, most were too polite to ask. The true explanation was more compelling.

When his ship was torpedoed, Tom, in desperate haste to abandon ship, slid down a rope towards the water, badly skinning his hands. Lifeboats had been launched but were already full. He had to tread water while holding on to the hawsers loosely draped around one of the lifeboats. As his hands were raw and bleeding he could only hold on with his teeth. In that nightmarish situation and ice-cold water he wouldn't have noticed his mouth being chafed by the sea's constant movement. As he said of another occasion, his memory of the horror was deliberately wiped clean from his mind. However he did remember the strange apparition of his long-dead grandmother walking towards him on the water, and his exclamation, 'O Granny, you'll get your feet wet!' She called back, 'Tommy, keep the men together. You'll be rescued in half an hour.' He obeyed her direction, calling his men to stay close, telling them that they would be saved in half an hour. And indeed they were.

While convalescing with the crew in hospital, he asked one day, 'Did you hear me call to you, when we were ditched, "stay together lads, we'll be out of this in half an hour"?' 'Yes, of course,' they confirmed. Puzzled, he pointed to his damaged mouth. 'How do you think I spoke?' he asked. Such was the bond between them in that dire situation that spirit had transcended physical distress. Tom was as awestruck as they were. Later he said, 'You can be very near to death, and know you are, and you can also *think* you are very near to death. It is far more painful and difficult to *think* you are near to death – narrow escapes happened so frequently.'

In between these stressful times at sea, when he was in port, there would sometimes be an unexpected knock at Tom's cabin door to announce someone from the Church, his visit prompted by the caring Bishop Stannard.

*

After the war Tom stopped going to sea, his decision prompted by his involvement with a girl he nearly married and by his being offered a better job. Later he met Patricia Matthews, whom he married on 24th April 1948.

The newlyweds stayed with Pat's parents in London until they found a flat near Finchley Road tube station. When this proved unsatisfactory, and after another spell with Pat's parents, they found a house in Edgeware.

Details of Tom's activities during this period are scanty. It was a time of political change, the introduction of nationalisation, health care for all, and a whole raft of new shop-floor reforms. Trade unions were influential and active. Tom was in the midst of it all. Pat recalls his working at Fulham Power Station, also at a power station in Kent; he was also briefly employed in a chocolate factory, and spent some time working in Ruislip in Middlesex. He finally settled with Handley Page, the aircraft manufacturers. All this time he was busy with Union work and he became Branch Secretary of the AEU in West Hendon. 'He was always on the go,' Pat recalls. When they lived in Hampstead he was closely involved with the Hampstead Labour Party which often met on a Sunday morning at Jack Straw's Castle, the well-known Hampstead pub. Pat remembers that Sidney Silverman[1] was one of his friends.

Tom attended Labour Party conferences and was no doubt well known to union and Labour activists. This was confirmed when IRIS – Industrial Research and Information Services Ltd, the industrial wing of Common Cause – invited him to stand as Divisional Organiser for North London. It is interesting that Vic Feather, the TUC General Secretary, had encouraged Common Cause to seek out and support moderate trade unionists 'to stand up against Communists and other militants of left or right fomenting politically motivated disruption or planning to do so.'[2]

Tom did not think he had any chance of being actually elected Divisional Organiser but was prepared to give it a 'bash'. He won by a single vote. This was in 1957. The Communists who dominated the AEU in North London were not amused!

CHAPTER 7

The Communist Threat

We must resort to all sorts of stratagems, manoeuvres and illegal methods, to evasions and subterfuges, so as to get into the trade unions, to remain in them, and to carry on within them communist work at all costs.

Lenin[1]

The fiercest struggle against Communism takes place within the trade unions themselves. It is here that the Red Fifth Column have their only real hope of disrupting and damaging the country... The Communists deliberately choose to undermine the unions to which they pay nauseating lip-service and which are strategically useful to them in the event of war, or civil war.

Cassandra, *Daily Mirror*, 13th June 1958

LOVE OF JUSTICE tends to foster love; hatred of injustice tends to foster hate: hate divides, love unites. The methods of Communist activists were certainly divisive. Their record at the ballot box was dismal so they targeted the unions, using the strike weapon. They set out deliberately to paralyse the state, believing the reins of power theirs to grab. They thrived on grievance, and management which was frequently insensitive and high-handed made things easy for them. Declining sectors of the economy — dockyards, coalmines, outmoded engineering works — were perfect targets. But few unions escaped their attention, certainly not the Civil Service and teachers' unions. Then there was the media, the perfect place to plant fellow travellers!

This was the post-war battleground in which Tom found himself at the front and all too often under fire. A frustrating factor was the general apathy of union members. This was the Communists' ally.

The *IRIS News* in September 1956 printed the following:

The success of Communists in securing positions at all levels in the TU movement is mainly due to apathy ... of TU members. The fight to preserve the basis of constitutional trade unionism, respect for negotiated agreements etc, must be waged on the factory floor and in TU branches ... Those who have experience know that the communist force, while small, is extremely active. There are no apathetic CP trade unionists ... They exercise an influence quite out of proportion to their numerical strength ...[2]

21

Tom faced bitter and devious opposition from the Communists, who were quite prepared to resort to dirty tricks. Frequently he despaired, but faith held firm:

> I fought Communism within the Trade Union Movement because they told me bluntly – and I had several Communist friends – 'we want to destroy the employing class, for industry belongs to the working class'. This is wrong, I thought. Industry belongs to God. It was what I'd learnt in Sunday school, what I'd taught at Bible class and what I'd worked out from the Bible.

Tom's troubles reached their zenith when he was elected, by that one vote out of seven thousand, as AEU Divisional Organiser for North London, a huge area stretching from Slough to Dagenham. His opponent had been a much-favoured Communist. Their frustration was explosive.

The *Reader's Digest* carried Tom's own words in September 1967:[3]

> I inherited an almost completely communist staff. Whenever I went to argue a case, I was accompanied by a communist convenor, chosen by the District Committee. Even when we won he reported back, 'Brother Chapman was totally inarticulate.
>
> They made the ridiculous charge that I was fiddling the books, which I easily disproved. My time was wasted fighting hopeless dismissal cases which the communists raked up. When I went to an unofficial strike at Ford's, the factory convenor refused to tell me where the meeting was being held.

The campaign against Tom Chapman was relentless. This from *The Star* of 10th June 1958:

> One non-Communist area committee man said: 'Whenever Brother Chapman visits our area to attend a meeting he is subjected to jeering and barracking from the time he enters the room. His word is rarely taken. He has been accused of untruth, and threats to kick him out of office are always being made.
>
> 'There are always a string of complaints made about him for not dealing with cases involving our members as the Communists think they should be dealt with. But it is plain that the attacks on him are always over cases which from a trade union point of view were hopeless from the start.'
>
> In one area of the Division an AEU member has reported that correspondence over union matters was asked to be sent direct to the private address of a Communist official rather than to the Divisional office at Tufnell Park. This appears to have been done so that the Communists could deal with disputes without Mr Chapman having knowledge of them.

This was confirmed by Cassandra in his *Daily Mirror* column on 13th June 1958:

> [In 1957] Mr Tom Chapman was elected a divisional organiser. He captured the job from Joe Scott, one of the most virulent champions of the Communist Party, by one vote.

From then on, Mr Chapman has been a marked man among the nest of Communists who run the North London Division. They deliberately set out to get Tom Chapman. They organised a plot and a dirty smear campaign to make his life, as a non-Communist official, quite unbearable.

In factory floor terms, they set out to 'do him'.

His files were purloined. Information was withheld from him and a staggering list of phoney union grievances and baseless complaints was thrust before him. A whispering campaign was set in motion, and he was barracked and jeered at meetings. Correspondence was diverted.

Having failed to keep Chapman out, the Communists waged a dirty campaign to destroy him in office.

Many viewed such stories as scaremongering, as seeing 'Reds under the beds'. Hugh Lunghi counters this opinion in *The Common Cause Story*:

After the collapse of the Soviet Union, it was the proud boast of ex-communist officials, and confirmed by Russian historians, that the Reds were actually right in the bed and being paid for being there by Moscow.[4]

The Communists' dirty tricks drove Tom to breaking point. They habitually kept meetings running late, hoping that he would give in to exhaustion and leave them free to their devices. He never did. He told how at times Pat would wait outside in the car. 'For goodness sake put me under a street lamp where I can read,' was her one request. She'd come well prepared with rugs and hot-water bottles. Her presence stopped the tyres being slashed or the car being scored – it had happened; and with his lady there Tom would hopefully escape physical violence. Some honour remained.

These were the days before clean-air regulations, when fogs were of the 'pea soup' variety. More than once Pat would have to walk in front of the car with Tom peering half blindly through the windscreen. Her patience and dedication was a wonder. She was out so much her mother began to ask if she ever washed up.

Communists dominated Tom's offices at Tufnell Park: no one would co-operate and telephone calls were often not put through to him. One caller that did get through was a Miss Glading, who shared her name with a prominent Communist. Tom tells the story:

I was so beaten and utterly fed up. Everything was going wrong. There were two telephones, one of which came to me via a secretary, who took care to filter out personal calls. She said I was out when I was in. One day the phone rang when she was not around and I picked it up. It was a female voice, quite angry. She said, 'Are you the Divisional Organiser?' I said, 'Yes, I am', and thought I was in for real trouble. She said, 'You're defending one of my employees whom I dismissed for being drunk and disorderly. He was drunk and disorderly, otherwise he would not have been dismissed, and it wasn't the first attempt.' I felt really sorry for the woman. I said, 'In the first place, you must realise that when a case goes to court, the Divisional Organiser only signs the certificate. He doesn't actually take up the case himself. The lawyers take over.'

Something in this woman's voice compelled me to believe that I should try and help her, so I said, 'Look, I'll come and see you. Where is your office?' She told me it was down in the docks. I knew how to go. I went there the following day and found her. She was a sweet lady, younger than me. As I was going in – I'd had a very tough fortnight – I actually fainted. That was the first time I remember fainting. When I recovered another man had joined her and, after some discussion, they said, 'There's a man you must meet.'

That man was Leon MacLaren, a barrister with knowledge of trade union law. Tom was desperate: the Communists were accusing him of sexual harassment – no doubt Party women were under Party orders. To make matters worse Tom's faithful secretary, who had been suffering verbal abuse (something she dismissed) felt compelled to leave when her boyfriend was threatened and roughed up. So, with nowhere else to turn, Tom took up Miss Glading's offer to visit the barrister's chambers in the Temple.

'Talk,' MacLaren said and for half an hour Tom did. When he had finished, the lawyer laughed heartily. 'Let's go and eat.' Off they went to Lyon's Corner House where Tom said they had a hearty meal.

Suddenly things began to happen. A new secretary was recommended and appointed, a willowy blonde named Barbara Beenham. She was Tom's 'secret weapon'.

Barbara, my new secretary, was wonderful. Not only was she very beautiful, but every time I attended a District Committee meeting or a Divisional Organisers' meeting – remember almost everyone present was a dedicated Communist – the remarks that were made about her simply floated over her head. She was cool, calm and collected. And she was so tremendously efficient. That was the thing that really mattered.

It was through Barbara that I met Colonel Whitehead, head of the London Employers. He confirmed what Barbara had discovered while going through the records – that the Communists were digging up all kinds of hopeless cases that had already been dealt with and lost. It meant that day after day the ordinary cases I took up were invariably concerning someone who had previously been tried by my predecessor and the London Employers and proved guilty.

Some of these hopeless cases, curiously, I won by tackling from a different direction. There was one man who had borrowed a tool. I eventually went to his house to find out what he'd used it for. He actually intended to do what I knew he would, as many others do, take it back next day. But he was caught with the tool on his person and he was rightly dismissed. I went back to the Employers and told them what had actually happened. After an adjournment they returned. 'We'll take him back. We accept your explanation.' That's just one example among many where I was able to help people.

The worst thing about cases that have already been dealt with was that the employer not only had records as to why a particular man had been dismissed, but invariably many previous ones where the same man should have been dismissed. That's where the difficulty was. Yet even there, I was sometimes able to get the job back where the Communists had failed. Very often I discussed cases with Barbara before we met the employers. This very wonderful young lady's expertise in picking out the odd point in favour of our client was tremendously useful.

Barbara went everywhere with Tom. Some of the venues were questionable but in her presence thugs who would have menaced Tom held back.

Tom also acquired another secretary, Oonagh. While Barbara was tall, Oonagh was short, but she was equally fearless and efficient. She was mostly occupied in the office at Tufnell Park. Tom now had two wholly trustworthy assistants. He was no longer isolated.

Meanwhile the Communists compiled a list of Tom's 'misdemeanours and omissions'. It was impossibly long and detailed and he was at a loss to know how he should respond. He took the letter to his barrister friend, who immediately dictated a reply. The gist was simplicity itself: 'Dear ... Thank you for your letter of ... inst, the contents of which have been noted. Yours sincerely.' Tom sent it off and heard no more.

Slowly the tide began to turn until it was the Communists who were under pressure. The press had a story and they were telling it in inch-high headlines. The *Daily Express* article by Trevor Evans dated 3rd November 1958 pulls no punches:

Sensational evidence against the Communists in the Amalgamated Engineering Union is to be published soon. It will be contained in a report on 'The Affair of Tom Chapman' and it will show the lengths to which Communists will go when thwarted.

PERSUADED

Chapman, formerly an aircraft fitter, now in his late forties, was persuaded early last year by a group of non-Communist members of the AEU to run for the job of North London divisional organiser.

It had been held by a Communist for more than 20 years and the Communist nominee was Joe Scott, who was expected to win.

But Chapman beat Scott.

And from that moment the Communists ganged up to make Chapman's life such a misery that he would throw in his hand.

He has said, 'No mean and despicable method has been overlooked in the attempt to remove me from office and so disrupt the democratic structure of our union.'

Every trick was tried. He was sent on fool's errands. Serious disputes were withheld from him until the last moment and then he was accused of neglecting his work.

His health began to suffer.

Then last June, Mr Percy Glading,[5] a Communist and office chief of the North London division, accused Chapman in the presence of two women secretaries of having indecently assaulted one of the women.

Chapman was aghast. When he protested his innocence he was reminded that his accusers were 'three to one'.

This weekend the woman involved,...who had been Chapman's secretary, announced there was no foundation for the indecency allegation.

She Resigned

In fact, she had pulled out within a fortnight of its being made.

But before she resigned the North London Communist leaders included the allegation in a series of charges against Chapman they made to the union's executive.

All this was done to counter Chapman's complaints giving details of the conspiracy 'to make his life a hell'.

So the executive appointed William Carron, John Boyd, and Claude Berridge, the Communist who represents the London area, to investigate.

One of the first things they did was to expunge the incident involving [the secretary] because of her prompt repudiation.

In their report to be published this month, I can disclose that Chapman will be vindicated and there will be a strong censure of the Communist 'plot' to drive him from office.

News of this has already 'leaked' to the North London Communists. At the last meeting of the union's divisional committee Mr William McLoughlin, an assistant divisional organiser, disclosed: 'I have seen a copy of the report. It is rubbish and contains lies.'

And Reginald Birch, North London's Communist chairman who is likely to be nominated to oppose Carron for the union presidency, is recorded in the official report of the meeting as having called Chapman 'a poisonous scorpion' and 'a little pigmy'.

Tough Fight

Obviously, the Chapman affair is only one incident in a campaign which could rock Britain's second biggest union. And it goes to show clearly how tough the fight against the Communists can be.

Looking back to this time, Oonagh recalled with amused satisfaction how she and Barbara had carried the divisional banner at a Labour Party rally. The Communists viewed this with clear resentment: how could two middle-class women carry the workers' banner? There were catcalls but they were not so impolitic as to snatch it from them.

Ray Cross, a life-long trades unionist, who became assistant to Jim

Conway[6] and later worked for Common Cause, maintains that Tom was 'probably the first to take on the extremists and defeat them at their own game. Tom's strength was in his Christian beliefs.'

Now here is a story worth recounting, one which shows Tom's honesty and strength of principle when he was Divisional Organiser. Tom begins:

There was a case concerning a convenor who was a dedicated Communist and whose employers were desperate to be rid of him, for he was always causing trouble. The convenor had called a strike, so I went to the factory concerned to investigate, for the convenor had been sacked.

He had called the strike at about two o'clock in the afternoon. I got there at about five and went straight to the toilet and in there was the charge-hand who had got the convenor the sack. The charge hand was jubilant: 'We've got your biggest enemy. We've got him for sure. He tried to strike me.' He added, 'What can you do? You can't defend a man who struck his charge hand, can you?' I said, 'Well, we'll discuss it with him.'

So I met this Communist later on and asked him what it was all about. He explained that he hadn't hit the man at all. He was carrying a template that was about six foot long and as he turned around the charge hand walked into it. He said he was sure — and I believed him — that the charge hand had deliberately walked into it and then accused him of striking him with the template.

I had to make up my mind whose side I was on, for I was convinced and I still remain convinced that the Communist had not deliberately struck the charge hand. I weighed it up and I put the whole case to the tribunal. 'A man who has been an experienced trouble-causer and a dedicated Communist, as well as being an experienced negotiator, would never dream of hitting anyone at all. Therefore, I'm convinced that there's no truth in this charge whatsoever.' And they said, 'Well, he says strike.' So then, for the fourth time in my life, I called an immediate strike.

We went as far as York. To go through Trade Union negotiations, you begin at the floor level and then you go to the district level and then to York. At York the final decision is made.

Tom's stance was not popular with the management: he was depriving them of a heaven-sent opportunity to rid themselves of a known troublemaker:

Now while this was going on, this 'piece of work' I was defending was actually being employed by the Communist Party to attack me in my next elections. He was fighting me all the way and here I was backing him all the way because he was in the right so far as his conviction was concerned. That he was attacking me was of no importance. He couldn't understand this at all, which is why I made one friend in the Communist Party, for when it was all over he came and shook my hand. He said, 'I've been fighting you with everything I've got and not once have you used it against me.'

That's the task of a Christian. He does his job and he defends the right to the last, as a trade unionist must. I have made more friends among employers by sticking rigidly to my code of truth than ever I would have done had it been anything else.

Despite Tom's fair-minded attitude, he was defeated at the next election. Doubtless the Communists and their militant army were determined not to lose to him again.

Tom was now forty-six. It was time for a new direction.

CHAPTER 8

The Mantle of the Church

Freedom, Fellowship, Service – these are the three principles of a Christian social order ...
Archbishop William Temple[1]

WHEN TOM CHAPMAN was representing his AEU members, conflicts of interest were common. As a trade union official he was duty bound to defend any man he was representing even if the facts of the case showed that he was actually guilty of a misdemeanour or shoddy workmanship. So what was he to do? He would pray for clear direction. Simplistic self-deception, the cynical might say, but when an open heart is not encumbered by the chatter of the ego, answers come. Yet Tom would never have taken such grace for granted.

Such dilemmas disappeared when Tom failed to be re-elected as Divisional Organiser. Now he needed new employment worthy of his strengths: it was the Church that came to his rescue. Tom writes:

In 1959 the Church Assembly adopted a report – The Task of the Church in Relation to Industry – which meant that, for the first time officially, the Church had accepted its responsibility in regard to the working life of the nation, a responsibility which up to that time it had shunned. Indeed, the record of all the orthodox Churches throughout the industrial era had not been good, and it had rested with individual Christians and men of goodwill, working alone, to succour those who suffered injustice and oppression in the industrial field.

The report allowed for the setting up of an Industrial Committee together with a Secretary and a Liaison Officer under the Board of Social Responsibility.

No one could have designed a better area of employment for Tom. He was advised to apply for a position the Board had advertised in *The Times*. He did apply, and to his surprise was contacted by the Board's Secretary, Professor A.E.O.G Wedell. Tom's own words are colourful and disarmingly direct:

I met Professor Wedell, a charming young man, who invited me to attend a conference of the Board of Social Responsibility at Ripon Hall, a theological college in Oxford.

It was a very beautiful May morning when I drove through the lovely town of Oxford, but for me the entry into Ripon Hall Theological College was literally an

29

entry into another world. A calm peace greeted me as I entered a long lane through a beautiful garden to the portals of the college, the first college I had ever entered in my life. What a contrast to the world that I was used to – like chalk and cheese.

I was greeted cheerfully by a clergyman, who obviously knew my name and was invited to sit on a long form. I was given plenty of time to think things over. I thought, how stupid to come here, to work for whom? I was not quite sure. I had never even heard of the Board of Social Responsibility. I knew what the Church Assembly was, but I had only met two bishops in my life. One confirmed me, and I had served for the other. Someone then told me that it was not the whole Board, but it was the Industrial Committee whom I would be meeting. Well this is more in my line, I thought. At least they will understand about industry. I became a shade happier.

A door opened in front of me and there was Professor Wedell. He smiled, but called in one of the clergy. I sat wondering. At first I thought, shall I go away? These people can't possibly want me to work for them. No, I must wait and at least behave with dignity. I had a lot to give to the Church and I sat there dreaming of the opportunity of telling a lot of clergymen what it was like, (a) to work on a factory floor, (b) to live on that kind of wage packet, and (c) the many battles that a Christian had to face. I had learned about most of them over the past ten years.

Out came the clergyman, smiling. Now it was my turn. I liked the way Professor Wedell made me feel quite happy with his remark, 'Don't worry. Just walk in and sit down where I show you.' I entered a large hall. There were about fifteen people sitting in a circle. I saw a bishop at the top, and there was a chair vacant for me opposite. He smiled and seemed a nice old chap. I looked around. I saw two gentlemen I had met before, General Sir Brian Robertson (later Lord Robertson) and a clergyman, Stephan Hopkinson. I did not know any of the others. Some faces had smiles on them, others were deadpan. I was very nervous. How stupid to apply for this job; this was not my field. Then I heard the still small voice that had said to me so many times in the past few years, 'Have a bash,' and I sat more upright. In a kindly voice, the Bishop of Sheffield asked me to say what I thought of working in the Church. My instantaneous reaction, was to say, 'What a huge question. Where do I begin to answer?' and then I suddenly felt impelled to tell them just why I felt I should work for the Church.

I remember that speech, probably more than any other speech I have ever given in my life. Perhaps it was the sense of hopelessness that rid me of my fears. For, certain I would fail to get the job, I spoke freely: 'Gentlemen, for many, many years now I have been wanting to tell someone in authority in the Church what ordinary people think of them – the Conservative Party at prayer. If I had the chance to work for the Church I would alter that. I would make people realise that the Church was for all people everywhere and was concerned with all people.'

Tom then told of his early years as a Sunday school teacher, his work as a trade union leader and the need for the presence of the Church in the shop-floor world.

I looked around again, at one or two famous faces, faces of people I had recognised on the other side of the fence, and I thought to myself, Tom, you'll never get this job, so use what time you have got to tell them just what you think – and how I enjoyed it! I laid my soul bare, telling them what I would do if I got the chance to really work for the Church. Then I breathlessly stopped, I think in the middle of a sentence. I looked around and there were stony faces, one or two smiles. The Bishop smiled, and asked if anyone had any questions. No one asked a single question. Then in a quiet voice the Bishop said, 'Thank you, Mr Chapman. We will see you later.' I walked out with a curious and almost absurd relief at having apparently lost a job. Of this I was sure. There was no doubt about it. But I had told them what I thought and what was more I thoroughly enjoyed doing it. I had done it without any fear whatsoever.

I remember walking around the grounds, where I met a sweet old lady. She said to me, 'How did you get on, Mr Chapman?' and added, 'Walk with me around these lovely grounds and tell me all about it.' It never dawned on me to ask her how she knew my name. We walked slowly and I enthusiastically went over the whole story, and then someone called us in to lunch. I sat in the lovely hall. It was very beautiful – a baronial hall, I thought. We were given a sherry. One or two of the gentlemen said kind things about where I had come from, Barrow. Someone said that he had heard of me before, but there was no mention about whether I had got a job or not. Then, when we stood around the table for grace, I noticed my sweet old lady standing next to the Bishop. Later I asked Stephan Hopkinson who she was, and was told that she was the Bishop's wife.

Now he had really done it, thought Tom, remembering just how frank he had been. However, he had enjoyed the lunch and the company; it was a wonderful experience.

Lunch ended. I was asked to wait. I waited with the lady and apologised to her, but she just laughed and said, 'Don't you worry too much.' She must have been in her seventies but the beauty of her youth still shone through. She was a wonderful woman. She talked as we walked about the grounds, but never mentioned the job at all. Then her husband the Bishop came out and said, 'Mr Chapman, we want you to come and work for us. We will discuss the salary. We want it to be whatever you got in your last job. Let's talk about your terms of reference some other time.' With numbed shock, I realised I was now working for the Church professionally, and I thanked God there and then for this wonderful opportunity.

Tom realised that some would view him as a capitalist stooge: it would be his job to persuade them otherwise, that working for the Church would mean upholding trade union principles. 'I arrived home,' Tom wrote, 'parked my car, a bewildered but happy man, that all the years' training that I had received was about to be put into use.'

The next day he attended the main committee of No. 8 Division of the Shipbuilding and Engineering Workers' Union; he still held the office of Secretary. As I looked around the room I saw *not* the Bishop of Sheffield but the General Secretary of the Sheet Metalworkers' Union.' What a different world – but was it? The General Secretary had been Tom's friend for many years; they were both Christians. Tom compared him with the Bishop – the only real difference was the accent.

Meanwhile, back at Tufnell Park the Communists were elated. In two weeks they would be rid of Tom. Once again North London would be their 'little Kremlin'.

*

Tom Chapman took up his new position on 1st July 1960.

It was a beautiful summer's morning as I travelled in the car from Edgware to Marble Arch, then down Park Lane, past Buckingham Palace, along the Mall and round Trafalgar Square. There was the difficulty crossing the lights into Whitehall, after which I continued on towards the House of Commons, turning right and then left into Deans Yard. Easing the car forward under that lovely archway, I stopped.

An angry-eyed uniformed man approached and demanded where I thought I was going. I told him I had just started to work at Church House. I said it very proudly. He reacted aggressively, 'You're not going through this archway without a permit. Who do you think you are?' I remember saying to myself, 'Oh no, not again.' This was how I began at Fortess Road, Tufnell Park, the very first day that I began my work as a Divisional Organiser. Then I was scared; now I was angry. I said, 'I am going to work in that building over there.' He said, equally angrily, 'You're not taking the car through here.' What a beginning! I said, 'Where do I go? What do I do with the car? That's where I work.' This gentleman of the Church said in no uncertain terms what I could do with the car! 'I will not allow you to pass through this door.' Boy, was I angry. This man was not a Communist; he was a uniformed Church employee using his authority as he was entitled to. That made me even more angry. So began my work at Church House. I backed out and eventually found somewhere to park, angrier than ever. So instead of a tranquil start to the work for Our Lord there was a very, very angry sinner demanding a permit from Mr John Scott, then the General Secretary of the Church Assembly as I discovered later! He was very, very charming and in an hour I had a permit to put the car in Deans Yard. I was to find that this permit was worth its weight in gold. The sequel to the story was that the beadle at the gate and I soon became very good friends, and remained so until he retired, and his successor was my friend as well. But it was not a very good beginning to my dream world of working for Christ in Industry and the Church, the union of the two.

Tom was introduced to Professor Wedell, whom he thought a brilliant young man with drive, yet very kind. After a cup of tea, Tom was shown to his own office. He described it as large and sumptuous, with two windows looking out into Marsham Street, two generous armchairs, a desk and a well-stocked library. The desk was free of paper. This seemed symbolic. This was a new venture: his was an unproven role, a search for usefulness. It was daunting yet challenging. Professor Wedell suggested that he think things over for a day or so, after which they would talk. An excellent idea, Tom thought; a novel one after the last frantic years.

Tom's whole working life had been a living example of Christian witness in the workplace and the role of the Church in industry was to him a burning issue. Somehow the Church needed to guard its essence and traditions while reaching out to people on the factory floor, presenting itself in a way the workforce could accept.

Tom had talent and experience, and his faith was strong – stronger than it had ever been. So what was he doing here in this paper-free office? Was he a stooge bolstering up the last bastion of capitalism? Was he merely placating that busy section of society which felt the Church should be doing something? Tom realised he would be dealing with Church Industrial Missions which had claimed publicly not to know this man Tom Chapman, the right-wing Divisional Organiser. The condescending, patronising way in which some of the clergy had responded when Tom told them who he was had been difficult to forget. This may explain why he was to be accused of causing trouble at some industrial missions: he was a sensitive but firey man. He concludes:

> The new role was an important one. I was to be, whether I liked it or not, whether the Church like it or not, the Ambassador for Our Lord Jesus Christ in a society that had not only rejected Him, but placed Him in the files of industry known as 'Charities, Covenants and Good Deeds Only'. To define the aims of my new duties was and still is simple, that all men and women in society shall love God and one another. Of course it is a platitude, but all platitudes remain platitudes until people do something about them, and it was my job to do something about it in industry.

Tom was no man's poodle but he was not yet formally established. It was not until two months later that his appointment was sealed with a three-year contract. However, from the beginning his energy and commitment were beyond question. In his new position he widened his contacts with Church and industry throughout the country while Pat, as ever, provided quiet background support; a packed suitcase was always ready.

> My task was to seek out and to help wherever and howsoever necessary the work in progress ... There were the organised missions such as Sheffield, Manchester and the South London Industrial Mission; there were the individual Industrial Chaplains in cities like Birmingham, Bristol and Coventry; there were the parish priests, ministering to their flocks in their places of work as well as traditionally in their homes; and there were the worker-priests ploughing their lonely furrows.

At Church House Tom acquired a new secretary, Margaret Bonstow, a godsend dedicated to his work. Her warm, open nature and touch of innocence were engaging and made her popular with Tom's friends, but she had no time for humbug. She was well-off and considered her work a vocation rather than a job. Tom had found another secret weapon.

This was a busy time for Tom. Sometimes he would go home just long enough to say hello to Pat and change his case. He travelled the country and, often with Margaret's support, would meet industrialists and workers in factories, or just as often in pubs. His report to the Board of Social Responsibility dated 14th June 1973 outlines his activities as Liaison Officer for Industry, beginning with those early years.

I was advised to start with a tour of the country and I visited many of the Industrial Missions, assessing the valuable work done by many of them and confirming in my own mind the magnitude of the Church's task in industry amongst management, clerical staff and manual workers. This tour raised many questions as to how the task might be more effectively carried out and various possibilities emerged. For instance it was immediately apparent that, despite their excellent work, the Industrial Missions were limited as to number and geographical scope and that an additional link with the Church was vital over a wider area of industry. I therefore set myself to the formation of groups throughout the country of which there are now several hundred.

Every group is different. Some are entirely made up of members of management; some are made up of shop floor workers and some of shop stewards, whilst others are of a particular industry or industrial area. Some of these groups meet regularly, others do not. All are unpublicised; this is essential, for publicity tends to attach a particular label to individuals which in the industrial field can prove harmful to their efforts and, in the case of a docker, is in some areas positively dangerous. The groups all have one factor in common and that is that through me they can look to the Church for guidance on any matter, be it the technicalities of the Industrial Relations Act, whether to stand as a shop steward, or whether a strike is justifiable. Every individual in every group knows that I may be contacted at any time of the day or night and that if I cannot provide immediate help, there is always a member of another group somewhere in the country who can. It is this sort of contact, based on complete mutual trust and confidence, which has made an immediate and practical link between Church and industry and which is greatly appreciated by those working in industry.

During my first year I was asked to produce some kind of newsletter giving as far as possible an unbiased view of the various problems facing industry. I saw the purpose of the newsletter to provide not only subjects for debate and discussion but also as a regular link between individuals and groups up and down the country. The first circulation was 50. To date seventy-two newsletters have been produced on a wide variety of subjects and the circulation has increased to over 2,000. Unions, employers, organisations and parishes frequently seek permission to reprint in their own journals and magazines and many letters of appreciation have been received.

These are formal words written for a committee. The deeper nature of his message was expressed in Tom's very being, in the love, fellowship and confidence he transmitted. His true impact cannot really be read in the awkward pages of an official text.

Some of Tom's groups were discussion groups, others were prayer gatherings; many were loose amalgams. In time it became the custom for them to come together in larger groups and ultimately in weekend conferences.

In the early seventies, however, the Industrial Committee began to question the nature of Tom's work and stress the need for communication. Were the Committee's work and Tom's work overlapping? Were they wasting scarce resources? Here was misunderstanding more than fault, the difference between a considered approach and one that was practical and spontaneous. Tom's was the way of the heart. He would have felt constricted by the analytical requirements of committee work. Over the years there had no doubt been a change in the Committee's attitudes. The membership was different too.

Tom wrote an eight-page report in June 1973 yet the following year the Committee was still complaining about lack of information, saying that people did not know what the Industrial Liaison Officer actually did. There were always 'the few', Tom noted, who opposed the Liaison Officer – 'small men' in his opinion. Their condescending attitudes were hard to bear, but Tom held his peace.

After fourteen years, however, the time had come for a parting of the ways. Tom's work was to be dissociated from that of the Board but the Committee were assured that his work would continue on a private footing. Tom left the Board of Social Responsibility on the last day of December 1974. The good wishes of the Industrial Committee were minuted and Tom continued to use Church House for his meetings. He was now sixty.

This could not have been an easy time for either Tom or the Committee. He was not a man to be ignored. However, he was now free to work in his own way, which he did not need to justify in reports. The future was exciting; his infectious enthusiasm is easy to imagine.

Less than a year after his parting from the Board Tom received a letter from Downing Street inviting him to become a Member of the Order of the British Empire in the New Year's Honours List. Clearly the Church had submitted his name.

CHAPTER 9

The Age of Strikes

If we equivocate between freedom and totalitarianism we will injure ourselves and the values which founded our [Labour] movement ...
We must never treat our members with contempt or distrust their judgement. We will have to understand that solidarity is not just the majority supporting the few but the few supporting the majority. We cannot claim to protect the weak if we ourselves endorse actions which inflict harm upon them.

Frank Chapple[1]

S TRIKES ENCOURAGED by Communist influence, especially wildcat walkouts, weakened post-war Britain. 'In 1993 Lord Scanlon[2] acknowledged that abuse of union power, more than any other factor, had been responsible for the destruction of the British motor industry.'[3]

Militant unionism was eventually confronted by the Thatcher government in the eighties and was seemingly laid to rest when the hollow edifice of the Soviet empire fell apart. Before this, in the heyday of their militant power, few would have guessed at the full extent of Communist infiltration. 'It couldn't happen here,' was the general sentiment – but it did. It was a true crisis in the nation's history, definitely a near thing, and the prospect of major disruption had been real.

The hard left chose their targets well. One was the nuclear submarine shipyard at Barrow-in-Furness. Tom was involved in the '68 and '72 stoppages, not as a trade union official but as a Church representative. The '68 strike was sparked off by a demarcation row described as a 'who tests pipes' dispute by the *North Western Evening Mail* of 11th December. On 6th September the *Barrow News* reported that the dispute had 'brought to a halt all fitters' work on the nuclear submarines *Churchill* and *Repulse*.' They also reported that Eric Montgomery, Barrow Secretary of the AEF, had asked the AEF national executive 'to declare black work on nuclear submarines all over the country.'

On 11th October a frustrated Vickers management put their case in an 'Advertiser's Announcement' in the *Barrow News*. They addressed a number of issues and on the matter of demarcation they said this:

36

Now we come to the demarcation dispute, and here the situation has taken on a Gilbertian atmosphere. We, as a firm, made two suggestions as a compromise, and let us not forget that, in total, we are talking only about six men, whether they be fitters, plumbers, coppersmiths, or any happy mixture of the three interested crafts. It is more than likely that when an arbitration court sits, the decision as to loading will be such that this strike has been provoked by whether or not one man held a Plumber's Union Card or a Fitter's Union Card.

The strike dragged on and in late November/early December Tom Chapman and a few friends spent the weekend in the town. Tom's friends listened, then asked questions. What was the strike about? They were specifically instructed not to take sides. They visited pubs and introduced themselves as representing the Church. On Sunday they attended various church services and later were received by the strike organizer. They listened to his deep resonant voice. 'A reasonable man,' they first thought. Then clichés began to flow, talk of 'warmongering imperialists' and the like. Still they listened and made no argument. They only questioned. Tom's work sought conciliation not controversy.

A number of Tom's young helpers were economics students from the school[4] in which his friend MacLaren was the leading figure. Some felt their presence had had little impact; Tom thought differently. Questioning what the strike was really about was potent, for in the mist of claim and counterclaim the cause had been forgotten. Tom believed that prayer, meditation and quiet listening helped to melt the harshness of distrust so that reason could break through. That someone had cared enough to travel up from London was also important; it was a long-drawn-out strike that was biting hard.

One intrepid soul found himself in a members-only union meeting and observed the tension in the hall. The chairman's first words were to ask everyone to move forward to allow more room at the back of the hall, although there was already ample space. Our observer wondered why. All obeyed and from then on the main speaker played his audience like a flute. His resonant words seemed reasonable but if anyone had the temerity to ask a question the chairman and the eight members of his platform party would point in unison – arms at full stretch – at the offending questioner. It was blatant intimidation to discourage the slightest criticism of the platform's line.

In his report to the Industrial Committee of the Board of Social Responsibility Tom wrote:

The strike, which has lasted many months before this visit, ended a month afterwards. The Barrow Group is greatly strengthened and one of its members is now on the AEF District Committee and able to make an invaluable contribution to reasonable and fair relations between management and men. Indeed there has been at least one occasion when strike action for purely political purposes would have occurred but for the efforts of the Barrow Group and this man in particular.

The plight of the ordinary Vickers employee caught up in this protracted stoppage was distressing. Strike pay was minimal; pitched against their instinctive loyalty to the union were the pressures of home. Certainly there would not be enough in their pockets for a regular pint: this was one of the first memories recalled by a veteran of the strike recently interviewed at a Barrow working-men's club. Probably most of the men had no wish to strike but, traditionally loyal, they obeyed their leaders. With the militants in control only a strong man could defy the platform at stage-managed mass meetings.

During the stoppage in 1972 Tom again journeyed north, receiving front-page prominence in the *Barrow News*, which described him as a special envoy of the Archbishop of Canterbury. This was again a serious situation: Vickers were threatening to close the Barrow shipyard. The dispute concerned boilermakers' pay and during its two months' duration it caused the lay-off of 8,500 workers. In recent years this strike culture had begun to seem remote but now public-sector unions are beginning to show a resurgence of militancy.[5]

CHAPTER 10

The Pilkington Strike

The condition upon which God hath given liberty to mankind is eternal vigilance ...
John Philpot Curran[1]

THE PILKINGTON STRIKE of 1970 should never have happened. Pilkington, a private family firm with a near monopoly in UK glass-making, had cared for their workforce and were well ahead of their time in the welfare facilities they provided. An appreciative union, the NUGMW (the National Union of General and Municipal Workers) were co-operative and had fifty-fifty representation with management on a Joint Industrial Council. Lulled by good relations, however, wage bargaining had become cosy and, although reforms were being considered, a low basic wage persisted. One man who was a shop steward at the time remembered as many as 217 differing rates of pay throughout the company. Such complications had not been rationalised.

The NUGMW were on such good terms with management that they had neglected union structures. Only one Branch Secretary covered 8,000 members in St Helens. In short, they were behind the times. The Pilkington board tended to ignore communication norms, confident that they *knew* their people, certainly the established ones. Pilkingtons *was* a family firm.

There was another factor. In the fifties, Alastair Pilkington (not a known relative of the family) and a group comprising management, scientists and the Chief Foreman Tom Grundy,[2] with a team of dedicated men, developed a new float-glass system that was to revolutionise glass production. Success did not come easily and for sixteen months glass from the first production unit had to be destroyed. Only a private company could have held out that long; the shareholders of a plc would probably have rebelled. Alastair Pilkington and his team who worked the plant did so for long hours with a selfless dedication. As one man put it: 'My dog bit me. He thought I was a stranger!'

In such circumstances the bond between management and men was close; as is the case with committed boffins, other matters tended to be secondary. Perhaps the Pilkington board was similarly preoccupied.

After months of effort they won through. The new float process was a world beater and Pilkingtons became a rapidly expanding multinational company. Sadly, some might say, the days of private ownership were drawing to a close, ending in the autumn of 1970.

In the excitement of developing the float process, and the company's rapid expansion, the low basic wage structure had been allowed to persist when it should have been upgraded. This blind spot cost Pilkingons, their employees and, indeed, the nation's manufacturing centres dear.

The unofficial strike took Pilkingtons totally by surprise. Strikes rarely occurred in St Helens but strike there was and its twists and turns read like a work of fiction, its heroes and villains etched against a swirling confusion of plot and counter-plot. Under the glare of publicity the official union, though reliable, appeared pedestrian beside the militant Rank and File Strike Committee made up of quick, clever, dedicated men. They had Communist and International Socialist backers, full of anticipation that the hoped-for moment had arrived: a class war that would smash the established order.

It all started on the afternoon of Friday, 3rd April. The previous day mistakes had been made in bonus payments, unfortunately not for the first time. A shop steward took the matter up. A heated argument developed and a four-hour deadline was given for the error to be corrected. Pilkingtons' lines of communication were not geared to such ultimatums, so the strike began.

The militants had their opening and exploited it to the full. Grievance followed quickly upon grievance until the original problem was overlaid. For a time the militant strike committee seemed unstoppable while the moderate NUGMW was sidelined, and the management dug their heels in. They would not be blackmailed. Return to work, they said, and then negotiate. This was exactly the excuse the militants wanted to justify continued action. The situation was serious as a protracted strike at Pilkingtons, supported by the blacking of imports, could quickly bring UK car production to a halt.

Tom Chapman knew the state of play but also knew from past experience that hard-left extremists were predictable, keeping to rules and plans and Party platitudes. A kind of humourless rigidity made them vulnerable to sudden change, and they did not know quite how to cope with ridicule. The moderates attacked and Matt McGrath, a tall goodnatured giant of a man, speaking on a NUGMW platform, listed the militants' 'achievements' in derogatory terms while repeating a catchy piece of doggerel about the cost of the hard left's 'revolution' to the average man each week. The militants threw pennies at him – distracting if not dangerous – but McGrath used the situation to good effect, implying to the crowd that the penny throwers were the ones who had smashed up Kirkland Street – the moderate union offices. The militants were losing their grip. One of their leaders who tried to snatch the microphone from McGrath, was shouted down. Finally a show of hands resulted in a 90% majority for a return to work.

The militants fought back, their pickets massing at the gates. The Rank and File Strike Committee organised another meeting and when the moderates, Matt McGrath, Ralph Leyland and Roy Horton courageously mounted the platform the militants dismantled the speaking equipment. There was pandemonium, screams of 'Let them speak' competing with 'Get them off.' Cleverly fronted by two women, McGrath was pushed off the platform into the midst of angry militant supporters. He was repeatedly kicked but managed to stay on his feet until policemen came forward to escort him.

For the militants this was bad public relations. Matt McGrath was popular. He was a decent man and no one liked the way he had been treated. The tide was turning yet the strike was far from over. Only stout hearts could brave the fury of the picket lines. The moderate Ralph Leyland and Harry Erlam were punched in the face, Erlam needing first aid. To get to work meant risking injury. Most stayed at home. A kind of civil war was raging between official union members and militant usurpers. Above all fear was dominant; anyone brave enough to stand against the hard left's will was under threat, and men were fearful for the safety of their wives and families. The situation had become a national concern.

The Pilkington family were aghast. Their pioneering glass-making plants were idle at huge cost to the company, St Helens and indeed to the nation's economy. Many of the workforce were still loyal; many were simply confused by all the claims and counter-claims. The militants sneered that workers had been 'drugged' by the nice, happy picture of a kind-hearted 'family concern', with an eccentric millionaire boss riding to work on a bicycle.[3] All this was unsettling.

David Pilkington, the Company's Personnel Director whom the strike had put in the hot seat, was a committed Christian. He chaired all the negotiations, with 'serious help' (his own words) from Vice Chairman Terry Bird. He was principled and his intentions were honourable; a less rigid negotiator would have been difficult to find, but the passions raging at the gates made him despair.

In March 1999 he committed some of his memories to paper. They begin with a telephone conversation with Tom Chapman.

'Hello.'
'This is Tom.'
'How are you?'
'David, you are in trouble.'
'I know that Tom!'
'David, you have lost the initiative. You have to do something.'
'What? Tell me.'
'Will you meet a group of my men who have been living in St.Helens for the last week? They will tell you.'
'Of course. When and where?'
'Tomorrow, Saturday afternoon, at your home.'
'Okay.'

I had met Tom Chapman at Christian Industrial Conferences and had great respect for his views. He was the first person to teach me that Christianity was not only about prayer meetings, choral singing, open-air preaching, or even churchgoing. More importantly, it was about justice and caring and action in the world. It was about establishing proper systems within companies, about organisations, about wage structures, about industrial relations. I had heard already from him about the people he had trained to go into the heart of a strike, find out what the real issues were and then attempt to build bridges between the parties concerned.

'Come in.'
'How are you?'
'Worried!'
'Well, we can help you.'

Into my home came six men. They were all professional people who had given up a week of their time to live in St Helens and go round the pubs and other meeting-places to see what were the real issues affecting the strike and what people really thought. So we sat and talked. They explained their role and came out with the stark message:

'You have got to make an offer.'
'But everyone's on strike and we don't negotiate under duress.'
'You need to regain the initiative. There are some people out there who want the strike to continue indefinitely.'
'What must I do?'
'Make an offer of £3 early next week.'

This was totally against management policy. We had said amongst ourselves, we know the strikers. We have worked with them over many years. They are good people. They don't want to be on strike. They will come back soon.

'They won't come back.'
'I think they will.'
'The tide is running against you.'
'What should I do now?'
'We must see the Chairman, Lord Pilkington. Does he go to church?'

'Yes, the Congregational Chapel in St Helens.'

'We will waylay him in the morning as he comes out of church.'

And they did! On Sunday afternoon we all met at Lord Pilkington's residence on the outskirts of St Helens while the case was fully argued. Lord Pilkington saw the point immediately. There and then he rang round his board and arranged a board meeting at 9 am the next morning, Monday.

So an offer of £3 per week was made and accepted by the main negotiating body, the National Union of General and Municipal Workers.

As an aside, it was interesting to note that everybody received £3 per week – management, staff, maintenance workers, as well as strikers, so that there would be no upsetting of differentials.

The main union accepted it on Monday afternoon, but a mass meeting of strikers four days later rejected it and the strike continued for a further three weeks. Eventually, with the help of Vic Feather, General Secretary of the Trades Union Congress, and a ballot organised by the clergy of St Helens, all the strikers came back to work on 20th May 1970.

There was another notable incident which occurred after the £3-per-week offer was rejected by the mass meeting. For the first time in its history Pilkington decided that it needed to communicate directly with its workers, individually and personally. How to do this? By letter of course. But how to keep the preparations secret for maximum impact? Virtually everybody in St Helens either worked for Pilkingtons, was inter-married or otherwise connected. We needed a totally secure printer and enveloping procedure. Here, again, Tom Chapman's people came into action. The letter was printed and enveloped in London. A car brought 8,000 letters back to St Helens, where they were posted.

Strikes are perplexing and depressing occasions. No one is sure – not even the strike leaders – what are the real issues of the strike. There are a hundred different opinions about its cause. There are plenty of so-called helpers who come flying in, like vultures – left-wing organisations, fringe religious groups, etc. Everybody is tired and emotionally drained. All this was my experience and it forced me back onto my deep foundations. I thank God for my faith which helped me to weather the storm and its aftermath.

And there was an aftermath. About five long-term major issues had to be faced:

The need for a new wage structure.

The need for new procedures covering industrial relations, grievance procedures etc.

The foremen wanted to be in a union.

Office staff wanted to be in a union.

The middle management wanted to be in a union.

And, in the short term, the breakaway union which the strikers had formed wanted recognition. The breakaway union picked on an issue and when the management refused to meet them they called a second strike in August 1970, three months after the first had ended.

A moment of truth! Would they hit the button again? Nerves on edge! Fingernails bitten! What would happen? What happened was that 600 out of 8,000 came out on a second strike. The remainder stayed solidly at work. Many of the 600 drifted back very quickly, leaving the real strike leaders of about 25 people still out. The real strike leaders left the company soon afterwards, encouraged within a legal framework by the management – they were sacked!

There were some moments when the management had to keep their nerve, particularly when the breakaway union tried for recognition. However, the management's nerve was never tested in the way that the nerve of the shop-floor workers was tested – standing in mass meetings voting against the breakaway union's proposals, threats to their persons, their wives and families, and perhaps, hardest of all, to lead early attempts to return to work through jeering, penny-throwing crowds of strikers at the factory gates. Many of these brave people had been trained and encouraged by Tom Chapman. These were simple, but vital, acts of bravery.

My own battles were simpler and called for easier and less direct courage. After the strike was over I had some late-night threatening telephone calls and two big picture windows in my home were smashed in after the breakaway union itself was smashed in August 1970. Luckily I was away on holiday with my young family and the damage had been righted before our return thanks to an alert neighbour.

The crisis was over, but much reconstruction had to be done. It may seem a funny thing to say, but in retrospect the strike was essential to the company and to the main trade union. Both had become complacent. Both needed to re-think their organisations and their industrial relations systems.

Pilkington had already started on this road two years before the strike with what was called the Productivity Programme, which aimed to look deeply at the wage structure (which we knew was out of date) and at every aspect of how the company was run. Unfortunately, too little, too late. However, some asserted that if we had developed a new wage structure at an earlier date it could not have been installed without causing a major strike.

Hence the sense of inevitability about the events that shook my life and many others to the bedrock of their souls. In such circumstances, faith may be discovered or rediscovered, and thus create a strong foundation to an individual's life.

To solve any conflict you have to have peacemakers or bridge builders. There have to be people of goodwill on both sides who have already built up links and trust and can inform each other what the real issues are and how the problem might be solved. Best of all, of course, is when the bridge builders are effective before the conflict turns to open warfare. Oh, for more such people in a hostile world!

*

The Pilkington strike stands as a warning to those who lead the nation's industry and commerce. It is dangerous to let the gap between the haves and have nots grow. It is dangerous to neglect people's needs or to let things slip, for in such situations the forces of disruption breed. A favourite quotation of Tom Chapman's was Edmund Burke's well-known warning that 'The only thing necessary for the triumph of evil is for good men to do nothing'.[4]

Today the tedium and hypocrisy of political correctness, the obsession with image, the suffocating burden of regulation and the general slide in standards may frustrate and perhaps alarm us, but we ourselves are hardly blameless. We demand our rights and forget our duties. We demand our freedoms and then behave with licence. We accept the daily wonder of creation and deny the Creator. This brings a shudder. In the words of Thomas Jefferson, 'I tremble for my country when I reflect that God is just and that his justice cannot sleep for ever.'[5]

CHAPTER 11

Rolls-Royce and Chrysler

It is not only individuals who must ... guide their policy or career by the principle of service; all groups of men must do the same. The rule here should be that we use our wider loyalties to check the narrower. A man is a member of his family, of his nation, and of mankind.

Archbishop William Temple[1]

IN APRIL 1968 the Labour government of the day announced their intention of giving Rolls-Royce launching aid for the development of the RB211 aero engine which the Lockheed Corporation had adopted for the Tri-Star civil aircraft. In October 1969 the figure announced was £47 million, 70% of a total estimated cost of £65 million. By the late summer of 1970 the launching cost had soared to £135 million. A further £42 million was secured from the Government. This was reported on the front page of *The Times* on 12th November, but on 26th January of the following year Rolls-Royce concluded that they could not continue with the project. A few days later, on 4th February, a receiver was appointed.[2]

Shockwaves ran out. This was Rolls-Royce, the national symbol of engineering excellence. For Derby, the home of the company, it was catastrophic.

Amongst Tom Chapman's papers is a typed message from the Revd John Oldham; it is in the third person[3] so may have been a Church House memorandum summarising a telephone message. It is dated 9th February 1971. (A of C is the Archbishop of Canterbury and TC refers to Tom.)

Communication between the Rolls-Royce factory and the outside world is dead. He (the Revd John Oldham) has been the only stranger allowed in the works. After attending a mass meeting, he has reported that –

1. A coach load will be coming to London on Thursday for the debate in the House of Commons, headed by Charlie Hunt.[4] They would like to see TC.

2. A request was received from the union that TC approach the A of C. It is not just a question of salvaging RR but of rescuing a city. The future of the British aircraft industry and the credibility of Britain abroad depend upon the keeping of the RB211 contract. The unions are looking for a lead from the Church.

46

There is an entry in Tom's diary for 11th February which reads 'RR, H of C'. It seems certain that he was present at that marathon debate which started at 4.30pm and ended after 4am the following day. He would no doubt have met his Derby friends and MP contacts. In the debate there were no strict party lines. MPs were concerned for their constituents and strongly pressed their case. One might say, in the words of Micha, that they were trying 'to do justly and to love mercy', for the situation was desperate. Philip Whitehead, MP for Derby North, painted a bleak picture:

Over the last week my hon. Friend the Member for Derby South [Walter Johnson] and I have seen a town facing a catastrophe. Derby is the headquarters of Rolls-Royce, and a labour force of about 25,000 people is faced with massive redundancies if the RB211 project fails. There is at the moment taking place in Derby a meeting of one hundred firms of unsecured creditors who have not been paid by Rolls-Royce and who are owed sums ranging from millions to £10,000 or £12,000. Many of those firms cannot see their way to paying their bills to the end of this month, in some cases even to the end of this week.[5]

A few months before, The Times leader had stated the case for intervention for practical reasons:

An aero-engine manufacturer, with the expertise and success in world markets of Rolls-Royce, is too valuable an asset to be thrown away in subservience to some ill-defined philosophy of non-intervention.[6]

However, Government intervention on the scale required would mean painful rationalisation. Tom reported to the Industrial Committee of the Board of Social Responsibility:

The collapse of Rolls-Royce was to the people of Derby as stunning an event as the most awful natural disaster, and it was into this atmosphere of disbelief that I was called by my Derby group. Many of the members of the group were highly skilled technicians who, overnight, found themselves, through no apparent fault of their own, parties to a great personal, social and national tragedy. What could be done for them? It appeared to me that the real concern of the Church at that moment of crisis was somehow, firstly, to lift the deep despair of the men by showing them that their plight was widely recognised and, secondly, by the more practical means of a call for generous redundancy payments, plus the setting up of industry requiring at least some of Derby's world-renowned craftsmanship.

This manifest and genuine concern of the Church led directly to a request for an interview with the Archbishop of Canterbury from a group of Rolls-Royce workers, who regarded this meeting with him of vital importance, and I know that the heartfelt concern which he showed them had the most consoling and strengthening effect. Their case was further advanced when it became known that the men were working unpaid to keep the engine project alive until the Government was able to step in with financial assistance.

*

Rolls-Royce cars were manufactured at Crewe, where a similar melt-down situation was threatened. As in Derby, shop stewards focused on trying to save the company. Here they planned to use their own savings, and even take out mortgages on their homes, to buy up Rolls-Royce shares and halt the slide. Tom called in Roger Pincham, a leading City stockbroker, to discourage them from what would have been a futile sacrifice at a time they most needed security.

What a stark contrast to the wrecking tactics of the hard left unions. These Rolls-Royce men valued excellence and were proud of their contribution to a world-renowned company. Rolls-Royce Cars were taken over by Vickers. Change was inevitable, but the tradition of the company lived on.

*

In the 1970s car workers were among the best paid in the land but hard-left union activists exploited the vulnerability of men on the production lines and a desperate management was often forced to appease inflated pay claims. As soon as one walk-out was halted, another started up. As well as this, wrecking tactics at suppliers' factories such as Pilkingtons or Girlings (which supplied brakes)[7] could halt production lines throughout the country. Too often the government had to intervene with cash support to prevent shut-downs, as was the situation with Chrysler's Linwood plant early in 1976.

Prime Minister Harold Wilson claimed that his Government was not 'in the business of subsidising industrial disruption leading to permanent loss-making ... Its purpose is not to provide a cushion so that the industry concerned can continue to lie flat on its back.'[8] But it had little option.

Tom travelled up to Scotland on 3rd February that year. His diary tells the story:

Arrived at Glasgow at 9.30 and Linwood at 10am. Booked into the only hotel in town where I appeared to be the only guest. I travelled to the factory gates by taxi. There were few pickets on the gates. No one I knew. There was the obvious IS[9] having little effect. I later visited a nearby pub and had some discussion after I had bought a round. But the apathy was tragic. Telephoned all contacts in Glasgow. Little effect.

Wednesday 4th: Curious coincidence – the chambermaid on my floor at the hotel was the wife of an assembler on strike as well as their son. After persuasion I was

Stressful times for Tom Chapman and his wife Pat, November 1958

Act of Dedication

Bidding

Christ has many services to be done: some are easy, others are difficult; some bring honour, others bring reproach; some are suitable to our natural inclinations and worldly interests, others are contrary to both. In some we may please Christ and please ourselves; in others we cannot please Christ except by denying ourselves. Yet the power to do all these things is assuredly given us in Christ, who strengthens us.

Let us then, who believe ourselves to be so called of him, engage our hearts to
the Lord and resolve, by his help, never to go back.

Response

I am no longer my own, but thine. Put me to what thou wilt; rank me with whom thou wilt; put me to doing, put me to suffering; let me be employed for thee, or laid aside for thee, exalted for thee or brought low for thee; let me be full, let me be empty; let me have all things, let me have nothing; I freely and heartily yield all things to thy pleasure and disposal. So God help me, now and always.

Amen

Act of Dedication in Westminster Abbey
following a conference on 'Responsibility in a World Adrift', June 1971

Awarded an MBE in 1976

Attending first AGM of Graphic and Creative Arts Association, November 1981

Visiting the Kremlin, April 1993

Evening years: Tom and Pat

Tom's Vision, painting by Charles Hardaker

Portrait by Charles Hardaker

introduced to them both and as a result was introduced to several men who were extremely helpful and we discussed the full problem.

I spent the whole day with them and was taken to meet several others. The Linwood strike has very little to distinguish it from any other, with one exception – the ordinary rank and file striker I met was less interested in the strike than any others I think I have ever met.

What never fails to amaze me is how 'Big Brother' is able to take over so easily, but here more than anywhere else I have visited. When I did persuade my friends, some action was possible. We did a good job. The heaviest costs were telephone calls to London for which I paid. It was worth it.

Tom made no further comments in his diary[10] and in fact the strike ended the following day. The opening paragraph of *The Times* report of 6th February read:

Production was resumed at Chrysler's Linwood factory near Glasgow yesterday after 4,700 workers had voted at an early morning meeting to call off their week-old unofficial strike – a dispute that threatened to bring about the collapse of the American-owned motor company's £162m rescue deal with the Government.

CHAPTER 12

The Bridgebuilders

Truth alone is important in every place and at all times. Other things have their importance in their time and place, but they come to pass. Truth remains eternally present.

Words spoken in 1971 at a Bridgebuilders Conference in London and quoted at the beginning of the ECIM brochure

---

AFTER HE LEFT Church House in December 1974 Tom Chapman continued his work as before, with no extended holiday, no time off at all. He simply hopped off one bus and on to another – his own bus, but a registered charity with trustees. The European Christian Industrial Movement was born.

Tom assumed the title Secretary-General; the President was Dr Ronald Williams, Bishop of Leicester, described in an early brochure as Chairman of the Church of England's Board of Social Responsibility and the Archbishop of Canterbury's representative in Europe – apt qualifications for his new role. His presidency was evidence of continuing links with Church House.

With the help of a generous friend Tom had already in 1973 acquired a London town house, conveniently sited at 37 Westmoreland Terrace, Pimlico. The new house was essential for his work, especially after he left Church House, when the extensive basement was adapted for frequent group meetings. Speakers' groups comprised of young men Tom was training in the art of public speaking would meet there, but there were also a number of other activities.

The ECIM also had an address in Brussels, 91/97 Boulevard M. Lemonnier, the office of Verena van de Loo (now Watson). This contact was established in 1973, the year before Tom left Church House and the year of the first Brussels conference.

Conferences were flagship events in the ECIM calendar and needed considerable organisation. There were also Thursday lunchtime services in the City at St Vedast Church in Foster Lane, EC2. The presiding rector was the Revd Canon Gonville ffrench-Beytagh who, as Dean of

Johannesburg, had worked with young black people in South Africa. He was first imprisoned and then expelled for refusing to segregate his congregation.

An essential fixture in Tom's diary was the monthly meeting of his London Group, a faithful core of which were his economist friends, many of whom had been with him since the Barrow adventure. These meetings took place on the first Monday of each month at Church House, but before they started there were unofficial gatherings at the Vitello d'Oro restaurant in the basement of Church House. Tom had become firm friends with the family who ran it. A good number would gather for the pre-meeting meal and in his enthusiastic way Tom never failed to welcome those who joined the long row of tables. Those were enjoyable times.

Tom was kept very busy. He was sometimes invited to preach in the pulpits of clergyman friends who understood the power of his sincerity, as well as at lay gatherings. There were also his many groups and contacts needing attention. Doubtless over the years he had gained a reputation for being a one-man arbitration service – 'Ring Tom Chapman. He'll help!' In August 1977 Douglas Thomas[1] did just that. He writes:

During the summer of 1977 tensions arose between the Highways Operatives and my colleague's section concerning the running of their Incentive Scheme. Industrial action on a potentially large scale became a distinct possibility. My colleague and the TGWU Branch Secretary were not the sort of men who would consider 'giving in' in any way and we appeared to be heading for real trouble.

Although a reluctant union activist, I tried to play my part as well as possible, particularly as a peacemaker. A friend suggested that I approach Tom Chapman for advice, so I rang for an appointment.

When we met I gave Tom a brief description of the situation in Bromley, including my own views about the two main protagonists. I explained the need for care on my part, particularly as my colleague and I reported to the same senior manager who, I felt, was keeping a careful eye on me because of my involvement in union affairs.

No one at Bromley – councillors, senior managers, office and union colleagues – knew of my approach to Tom. It was kept absolutely secret from everyone. Tom told me he would check up on the TGWU Branch Secretary and let me know anything arising from his investigation. In the meantime I was not to worry.

We spoke on the phone a few days later when he had completed his enquiries. His words were, 'That chap (the Branch Secretary) is known as a 'Philadelphia Lawyer'. He makes up his own rules as he goes along.' Tom told me to let him know if the situation deteriorated.

I was left with the strong impression of strength and calmness. We had only met for about ten minutes and had only had a brief telephone conversation, yet all was under control. Indeed, the industrial relations problem dissolved and I felt very strongly that his influence had contributed to that dissolution.

In the early 1980s Tom was still visiting areas of conflict though almost 70 years old by then. Colin Crawford commented:

I did not know Tom very well and, indeed, only met him a couple of times, I think in about 1982/3 when I was the General Manager of Sealink at Harwich. I then had a very difficult industrial relations situation which was made worse by militant action. Tom turned up, out of the blue, and at first, I was a little surprised when I greeted him. I soon found that he was very genuine. He had been into the pubs and had been talking to those on strike. In coming to see me his whole purpose was to help to build a bridge and in no way to argue on one side or the other. He had no sense of criticism or condemnation of anyone. I was very impressed with a man who just wanted to give and did not want to receive anything except to listen and try to help.[2]

All this happened during the ECIM period, but what was the nature of this body and what were its aims? An extract from one of its brochures reads:

ECIM is a movement which seeks, through love, knowledge and wisdom, to serve the basic Christian principles and to build bridges between people of all nations, in their working, family and community lives. Our objective is to turn the hearts and minds of men and women to God, that they may walk in His ways, within the teachings of Our Lord Jesus Christ.

Defining aims was not enough for Tom Chapman. He had a vision: a tarred road, a gate ajar, a driveway leading up the hill to a small church. He told every detail of it to the painter Charles Hardaker; he was very definite about how it should be represented. The symbolism is plain: the open road and the gate ajar beckon the weary traveller to tranquillity and rest, but even here temptation lurks to trap the wayward. The ECIM is the open gate beckoning all, and waiting. There are no posters, signs or pointers, just a simple church and a tiny figure on the hill, pure white, the Good Shepherd careful of his sheep (see Plate 7).

CHAPTER 13

Conferences

To this end was I born and for this cause came I into the world, that I should bear witness unto the truth.

St John 18:37

TOM CHAPMAN'S conferences were the jewels in the crown of his year. They were impressive occasions, but what were they about? What was their contribution to society? The speeches were invariably informed and erudite, even wise, but David Pilkington recalls that Tom would sometimes say, 'There's something missing,' a gap, a jigsaw piece not in place. It was Tom's gift to sense the atmosphere and then adjust. So what magic was he hoping for? He wrote, after the 1979 Westminster Conference:

The greatest contribution of a conference to the world is the intangible force of the power of love that builds up from the moment the first guests are greeted by their hosts and continues to grow until the Blessing forty-eight hours later.

With that Blessing I always sense a tremendous burst of the love generated into the atmosphere. It is written that science has armed man with immense potential power; but however great that power may be, it is minute in comparison to the power of love that man already possesses but has to learn to direct. These are moments when we succeed.

This was the sustaining power, the inspiration that Tom Chapman sought to foster: the power of love – God's love. This was the grace that he was always seeking, the strength that comes from peace and deep tranquillity. On the surface, Tom was at times anything but tranquil because of the pressures of organising the conference. His eyes would be watching, clear and very alert – the discerning seaman at the tiller of his conference ship. Timothy Glazier, Tom's valued helper at the conferences, is full of praise:

I have always felt that one of Tom's great skills was that of orchestrating the dynamics of conferences – meeting people as they arrived, setting the scene on the Friday night, keynote speaker(s) on Saturday morning, groups after tea, conviviality on Saturday night, strong spiritual input on Sunday morning, followed by the reports from the groups and the final session. By this time everyone had picked up the strong impetus of the event and were 'changed people' carrying a new energy back into the workplace. I have never known anyone with that same skill. It was a wonderful formula and it invariably worked.

I was always amazed by his 'certainty' about how things should be done – this seemed totally intuitive, although it was obviously guided by experience as well – but woe betide if one tried to go against that and do things differently because of intellectual considerations! I was also amazed by his courage and conviction. Every conference was a challenge and required an extraordinary confidence in his own judgement to arrange and carry through. Yet, before every event he would lose his nerve and get worried about whether anyone was going to attend. This was where Margaret Bonstow was always so good at reassuring him.

In 1979 Tom wrote a brief sketch of the year's conferences which gives something of the flavour which permeated these events:

The highlights of the year must be the three main conferences. In January was the Scargill Conference in Kettlewell, Yorkshire, during the heaviest snow-storm in the area for twelve years! Seventy-six managed to arrive, but credit must be recorded to fifty and more who tried and failed, having to turn back, some having got within ten miles when the police warned that it was unsafe to continue. Their endurance and tenacity was more than a contribution to the theme of the Conference, Towards the Eighties. It was a practical example.

The Antwerp Conference in June was attended by twenty from Britain and the theme was What can we do today to prepare for tomorrow? – chosen by the Revd Bill Gowland, President of the Methodist Conference. For me the highlight was not only the welcome given to us once again at the convent, but the loving, welcoming manner in which we were accepted into the homes of our new Belgian friends.

Millom Town Council in Cumbria (near Barrow) presented the Movement with a beautiful scroll to remember the October Conference. The town provided the brass band which enriched the whole proceeding, culminating with music to end the Westminster Abbey service at which almost a thousand were present. This conference had a galaxy of speakers: Sir David Nicolson,[1] Sir Patrick Dean,[2] Jack Peel, CBE[3] Dr Sergei Tarassenko,[4] under the chairmanship of our President, the Rt Revd The Bishop of Bradford. The theme was Bridgebuilders – towards the Eighties.

The conferences took considerable organisation and also, as Timothy Glazier emphasised, courage and conviction. It was little wonder that Tom had last-minute jitters.

Sergei Tarassenko, when asked for his impression of Tom, replied succinctly, 'He was a sincere man – a fighter. He didn't mind taking risks and he didn't take cover.'

Roy Calvocoressi, Founder and a Director of the Christian International Peace Service,[5] described Tom as 'electrifying'. Jim Chivers, then a technical representative with Shell Mex and BP Ltd in the Liverpool area, said that Tom introduced the word 'love' at shop-floor level to some of the hardest men you could meet. He 'genuinely tried to put into practice what he preached.' Jim remembers Tom's 'bounce'; he 'never operated flat-footedly. Exuberance, enthusiasm, strong feelings were part and parcel of his *modus operandi*.' Jim Chivers first met Tom at a Scargill Conference in 1972:

One instance comes immediately to mind. On Saturday afternoon, at Scargill, we used to go for a walk on the moors – or was it the dales? It was at the time that there were strikes in the transport industry over pay claims.

Now I had a connection with management, although over the six years in Liverpool I think I saw as many examples of bad and corrupt management as of utterly destructive union intervention. Both were prevalent and fed on one another.

Anyhow, on that afternoon I had a wonderful chat with a man about my own age. We shared our Christian background and talked about the speakers we had heard and how good it was to stand back and take stock. After some considerable time we came round to work. It turned out that he was a driver for a Shell subcontractor and had we met on the yard there was no possibility in that climate of us being anything but 'enemies'. I wore a suit and he had overalls. I was white and he was blue collar! We stopped on that Yorkshire hillside and looked at each other with our duffle coats and realised what a chat could do, especially with no preconceptions. We also probably had a pint together later. That was bridge building.

Jim Chivers pays tribute to a good friend of his, an ardent Tom Chapman supporter, the late George Ward:[6]

My first recollection of George was at Scargill when he made an intervention from the back of the lounge in that wonderful basso profundo voice. It came as a result of people saying that Christians do this and Christians do that and George bellowed out '.. and People of Goodwill'. George as a Quaker was given to action based on faith and never discounted anyone on the basis of a label.

Charles Hardaker, who painted Tom's portrait in 1976, related how Tom asked for his likeness to be in 'Churchillian mode'. He wanted it to be 'forceful, almost pugnacious'. Was this to emphasise that love, the bedrock of his life, was never to be viewed as sentimental? (See Plate 6.)

*

Max Baldwin was in his mid sixties when he first heard about Tom's conferences. Parallel experiences drew the two men together. Max had known extreme poverty as a boy; as a young man he had joined the Royal Navy, becoming an engineer. During the war he served on the Tobruk supply run where life expectancy was, to say the least, low. His ship was later blown up but he miraculously survived, although badly injured. Thereafter he lived with three contracted vertebrae. His naval engineering qualifications were not recognised after the war so he turned to market gardening, selling his produce from a mobile shop. It was hard work he little cared for. He retired early and was elected a local councillor, a thorn in the side of corruption.

Max Baldwin never missed one of Tom's conferences, until illness intervened. In the late nineties his daughter, the Revd Mrs Maxine West, recalls Tom's confiding: 'I've been talking to your father this morning.' He did not elaborate and she did not probe. It was very strange, however, for her father had died in 1974. Tom had said something similar once before. 'He often seemed to be on a different plane,' she commented; she thought his visionary quality very strong. This is interesting because Tom was anything but fanciful. His feet were very firmly on the ground.

*

Tom Chapman had good reason to be practical: experience had been a hard, uncompromising teacher. Do-gooders and one-idea fanatics were for him tedious distractions, but there had also been demonic forces opposing him.

Once he was asked to see a deeply troubled man. His natural inclination was to help but on this occasion his suspicions were aroused. Sensing something was odd, he took two precautions. He insisted upon meeting the man in the chapel at Church House and he asked a resourceful young friend to accompany him. The highly agitated man they met was black, not in colour but in his being: he exuded an air of evil. Wild-eyed and dishevelled, he was powerfully built. Tom grabbed his arm and, pulling back his sleeve, he revealed what he had expected to see, the satanist's tattoo. He had had experience of such people before. Little was said. Tom held tightly to the altar rail and prayed. It needed all his strength to stand against the power that was trying to overwhelm him. It was like a medieval play in which the forces of light and dark do battle. Tom held firm and the man rushed away without a word.

Tom's young companion later explained that he had felt deeply polluted by the encounter and it had taken some time to throw off its effect. Tom showed no sentimentality. He would never have been a pliant tool or, in Lenin's cynical words, a 'useful idiot'. God was Tom's strength and love was his way.

*

Tom's contacts were numerous; his travels seemed continuous. He journeyed to Glasgow, Devon, King's Lynn, Liverpool, Ipswich, Winchester, Bristol ... the list goes on. He also flew to Northern Ireland to meet union leaders and members of the ecumenical Corrymeela Community,[7] some of whom eventually travelled to Brussels for one of his conferences. He and Pat went on holiday to Switzerland and Rome and later returned to both places – to Switzerland for a conference and to Rome to meet the Focolare.

Not long after the Portuguese Military Council allowed a democratically elected government to assume power in 1976, Tom went to Portugal, probably to help set up free trade unions. He also visited post-Franco Spain at the request of some employers.[8] It was feared that Spanish trade unions might fall to Communists. Pat recalls his going to Germany to visit coalmines. And there were his numerous visits to Belgium. The picture is of someone ever on the move. No horizon was too distant. 'He had tremendous vision,' Roger Pincham says; Christian Schumacher[9] emphasises his 'great courage and integrity'. Tom was someone to be reckoned with, a force made stronger by the fact that Tom was not 'for Tom'. His mission was to turn the hearts and minds of men to God. There was no time off; there were no frontiers.

Roger Pincham sees him as a naturally pastoral man to whom people easily turned for help, knowing they could rely on his discretion. People would ring up about losing their jobs, or about other problems – he even saved a marriage from failure. One caller rang at 4.30 in the morning and immediately Tom set out by car. He never talked about the incident.

An event which left a lasting impression on Albert and Audrey Sandbank illustrates Tom's unselfish care. They were on holiday in the north and, being close to the Chapman home, telephoned to ask if they might call in. Tom explained he was just about to drive to the east coast, but offered to meet them half-way, at Leyburn in Yorkshire, for a pub lunch, when he would explain the reason for his journey.

When they met, Tom told his story. An elderly lady had been fighting her local council – to the frustration of friends and relatives, for she had no valid case. In desperation someone who knew someone who knew Tom suggested that she phone him. It was true, Tom quickly concluded, that she had no case, but even though she was a complete stranger he felt he could not tell her that by telephone. He needed to see her. So there was Tom, a man in his late seventies, embarking on a near-250-mile round trip to do just that. He did not feel this to be extraordinary; it was simply what was necessary.

Tom was a very emotional man and his feelings were not always easy to contain. Timothy Glazier noted that 'Tom was very sensitive and could easily take offence,' and Roger Pincham understood that he found such reactions well near impossible to disguise. Love won, of course. It always did.

CHAPTER 14

Two New Unions

The acid test of mission is whether we can make the Christian Faith and practice relevant in specific situations.

Revd Bill Gowland[1]

WHEN TOM CHAPMAN was in hospital in Barrow, close to death, a number of his London friends made the lengthy journey north to see him. One was Timothy Glazier. He felt impelled to go: Tom and he were close.

'What kept you?' Tom demanded. The banter emphasised affection. Timothy sat quietly; nothing much was said in the companionable silence. After a time Tim put his face to Tom's, and left. Vivid memories of their friendship remain.

For years he had helped Tom at the conferences and the relationship was strengthened when Tom advised him on the formation of an independent union in the face of rival union opposition. This needed nerve and courage, especially from one unaccustomed to such rough and tumble. 'There is nothing quite like a court appearance,' Timothy said, 'to wonderfully focus the mind!' All this time Tom's strength and experience were invaluable. Without Tom, Timothy feels he would never have taken up the challenge.

My work with Tom led directly to my own involvement with the Trade Union Movement in the 1970s. The setting was this. New technology was entering the design, advertising and printing world to the extent that people could become what came to be known in the trade union field as 'kitchen sink compositors', i.e. setting type on your computer in your back room and thus cutting out the traditional trade typesetters. Unionisation in the print industry was virtually a hundred percent at that time, so the print unions began to realise that their members were not only losing work but that a whole new area of potential membership was growing in the design studios, advertising agencies and among freelance artists and designers. This affected the National Graphical Association, NGA, and the Society of Lithographic Artists, Designers and Engravers, SLADE. They became very aggressive in recruiting into these new fields and developed the techniques of 'blacking', whereby unionised printers would refuse to handle work that had not been produced by union members. This included illustrations for publications and advertisements in

59

magazines. The problem came into the public domain when a telephone directory, which should have carried drawings by Albany Wiseman, was printed with a blank front cover, and newspapers were printed with spaces where advertisements had been refused by the newspaper unions.

I was then producing advertisements for a number of clients and, although I was not directly affected, there was always the chance that my advertisements might suddenly be refused by a magazine. So, after discussion with Tom, I decided to join what was called SLADE Art Union, SAU, which SLADE had formed as a special branch of their union for artists and designers, with a nominal joining fee and few rules and conditions. This would enable me to have advertisements accepted should the situation arise.

I was aware that this was a monstrous situation and, after joining, soon met up with other disgruntled freelance artists including a South African who, having left his own country in disgust at apartheid, strongly abhorred any form of injustice. Soon a group of us were meeting together to see what we could do. I introduced them all to Tom and in due course about a dozen of us came together to form what we called the Moderate Action Committee. So that we could handle money, MAC, drew up a trust deed and hired a solicitor. Tom gave public-speaking training to one or two of the members and the all-vital instruction on meeting procedure. Then, when SLADE's governing body began to change the rules of SAU without reference to the members, we had our opportunity to take action. The South African and I acted as plaintifs on behalf of MAC and we took out a High Court injunction against SLADE to prevent them changing SAU's rules over the members' heads. Other High Court actions followed and we also lobbied Parliament. This led to the Leggatt Enquiry into Trade Union Recruitment Practices, which resulted in the foundation of the Tory Employment Legislation on these matters. So, effectively, our little group was instrumental in changing trade union law – another instance of Tom influencing a course of action in a way that no one could have envisaged.

Whilst not directly involved, Tom was undoubtedly our sounding board and inspiration throughout all this. Had I never met Tom I would not have become involved at all. Again, it was his inspiration which gave me the incentive and courage to take quite considerable risks. Had I not had these links with Tom and got myself involved it is unlikely that these successes against unacceptable trade union action would have been achieved. Once the Tories were in power the MAC was disbanded, but there was still the danger that the situation might once again be reversed. We therefore felt that a moderate and understanding union was needed, so those previously involved set up a new trade union called the Graphic and Creative Art Association, GACAA. Once again Tom helped us with this. We were a registered trade union, though with a very small membership, and Tom was President. The intention was to become a branch of Frank Chapple's Electrician's Union but that never happened and the GACAA remained in existence. In due course we deregistered as a trade union and now those of us who were involved just meet for a meal once a year at Christmas!

This is a case of good men doing something,[2] so that bullies did not march on unopposed. Tom said:

I am an old-fashioned trade unionist in one respect only: when I joined my union the Chairman of the branch was obliged to ask, 'do you join this union of your own free will?' This was and is an important question. Nowadays there are too many who say 'You join, or else.'[3]

Clearly Tom's readiness to help and advise made all the difference to Timothy and his colleagues; his mere presence had impact. John Lockyer,[4] a graphic artist well known to Timothy, writes: 'You have it or you don't. Tom Chapman did.' He adds that Tom was a realist, not a Utopian; his personal ideal was 'a prayerful life which governed all that he did'.

*

Then there was The Union of Bookmakers' Employees, TUBE. By 1971 the Betting and Gaming Act, which brought cash betting shops to Britain's high streets, had already been on the statute book for ten years. Many enterprising entrepreneurs, often new to bookmaking, made small fortunes and found themselves sitting on capital assets because limited licensing due to restrictions made their businesses very saleable commodities.

However the advent of the Betting Duty, and the certainty that it would increase, changed the situation. Also large groups with chains of betting shops strove for further market penetration. Locked in competition, they pushed up the going rate for the purchase of smaller businesses and their precious licences. Many independent betting shop owners grasped this golden opportunity.

One such was Ben Moody, who sold his chain of twelve shops but was careful to ensure that the buyer undertook to continue the contracts of his well-paid staff. However, it was not long before Ben Moody's people realised that they were running the most notorious shops in the new organisation, and suffering the most difficult travelling problems. The unsocial hours were especially hard on young mothers. These and other harassments caused many to leave; when they did, they were replaced by workers on lower salaries. Such pruning of labour costs was common practice.[5]

Ben Moody's former staff, furious at their new employers' breach of faith, approached Don Bruce, a director of the National Sporting League, an employers' association. He was so enraged he resigned his directorship to take up the cause of the employees. Don knew Tom Chapman and quickly got in touch with him.

I made an appointment with Tom and took a delegation to Church House to see him. They reported that they had been to Transport House to meet with the TUC but had been disappointed to discover that no help was to be expected from that quarter. Tom asked many questions, took a couple of days to consider and then advised that, in his opinion, they could go it alone and start a new union, although it would be the first new union for many years.

Tom advised that they would have to hold an inaugural meeting, one which must be widely advertised and at which it would be necessary to pass a number of resolutions. These he promised to draw up. In the event, a meeting was held in a Tottenham Court Road venue which was attended by over four hundred betting shop staff, with one or two employers' representatives and a few others on a wrecking mission! I was acting Chairman and Tom sat on my right, bringing his expertise to the fore when needed. After well over an hour he nudged me, got to his feet and said: 'In all my years as a trade unionist this is by far the best inaugural meeting that I have ever experienced. All we need now is to pass a handful of resolutions and elect an Executive Committee and let them get on with the job of looking after the interests of the employees in this new industry.' He was warmly applauded. The meeting proceeded in the desired direction and TUBE (The Union of Bookmakers' Employees) was born. Subsequently, Tom made himself available whenever his advice was sought, particularly by the new General Secretary, the Northern Organiser and other members of the EC.

In due course the union won two cases in the Industrial Courts. Once, when faced with refusal by employers to even talk to its representatives, the union successfully closed over one hundred shops in Liverpool, Leeds, Manchester and Glasgow. At a later stage, when under financial pressure, TUBE's Executive Committee negotiated a deal with the then TGWU to take over and look after the interests of betting shop staffs. The firm of Joe Coral, with over 700 betting shops at the time, became completely unionised within two or three years of TUBE's formation. Without Tom it probably would never have happened.

It cannot be common for an employer to resign from an employers' association in order to help employees set up a union: it is a remarkable story. Honesty and common decency won through, but it took courage. The episode must have warmed Tom's heart.

CHAPTER 15

Education

People say to me, 'Christians must stand up and be counted.' I say to them, 'Why did Christians ever sit down!'

Tom Chapman, 27th November 1974[1]

EDUCATION has suffered greatly at the hands of political theorists. The post-war drive for fairness and equality was laudable: the old eleven-plus examination system had harshly divided children into the successful and the losers. Large comprehensive schools offering a wide range of opportunities were created. Some were fortunate in having strong head teachers, and worked well, but the blinkered way in which many were conceived caused much distress. Collectivised into catch-all units, many long-established and successful schools lost their identity and traditions. Unfortunately the trend was a 'dumbing down'. The well-known warning was ignored: 'You cannot strengthen the weak by weakening the strong.'[2] A new wave of private schooling was inevitable.

In the early seventies, when strikes were commonplace and the integrity of the state seemed to be in question, Tom called together as many teachers as he could. What he told them sounded almost like fiction: that a European far-left socialist group had targeted UK education and its Christian traditions.

It is doubtful whether they all believed these claims but some took the exhortations to heart and carried them to their union meetings. One became the union representative for his school and persuaded his own colleagues not to strike, though at a meeting of all representatives he was howled down. 'I was lucky not to be lynched,' he added. Another served on a small committee encompassing Southwark. Its members were mostly Marxists, but a likeable bunch. Having a clear agenda, they had a way of coupling two proposals in one resolution, one a perfectly valid proposal for better facilities, the other controversial – such as democracy for pupils – hoping the second would ride quietly through on the first.

Tom had warned the teachers that unpalatable propositions would be held back until the very end of a meeting, a time when only they, the left-wing activists, had 'stuck it out'. One of the teachers confirmed that that was indeed what they did.

A further problem was the Humanities Project: schools were fed information packs for personal and social education, including often questionable information on subjects such as sex. There were even extracts from Mao's *Little Red Book*, causing outrage at the time. Meanwhile religious instruction was under attack. A conspiracy theory? Perhaps ... or were the Reds already *in* the bed?

In April 1993 *The Common Cause Report* included the following:

Children's books have become a particular target of the Politically Correct. A survey of 100 children's authors by PEN, the international writers' body, brought to light the startling fact that upwards of sixty per cent of English children's authors had had their work censored on grounds of race, gender, class or religion. One author was told to remove a scene including a lawn because only wealthy people had lawns.[3]

Is common sense dead?

For Tom education remained an abiding concern, but it was a difficult area. Teachers were teachers. They only needed to be free to teach: most were reluctant union members. One senses that teachers' unions were not Tom's natural arena, though he loved children, and young men and women in the sixth form took to him, their open minds connecting with his clear sincerity.

*

Tom Chapman's conferences usually included a group discussing education, made up of teachers and others drawn to the subject. Tom of course emphasised that God's law was the real foundation of education. The ECIM Industrial Notes for April 1977 explain the background to these discussions.

Education must be concerned with the whole person – body, mind and spirit, and should meet the needs fully of each of these aspects:

That the stages of development of a young child to maturity are very specific and observable. That from birth until the fifth year is the stage of innocence and profound receptivity and the stage at which education commences and at which the child should be introduced to fundamentals that can enable the next stage to proceed. At this stage the teaching should be playful. The next stage, until the tenth year, is the stage of primary education in the sense of education in those things that are of primary importance to a child throughout his future life. In the next stage, to the fifteenth year, a child is ready to learn about the world and what the world thinks. Thereafter a young person is dependant on what has entered in these early stages and will be governed in his further development by the influences and education up to that point.

EDUCATION

The notes also listed questions for post-conference reflection. These have not lost their relevance.

1. What do you see as the true aim of education?
    To what extent do you see this aim being achieved in your country today?
    What steps would you consider could be taken to achieve that aim?
2. What are the responsibilities of the following towards the education of children?
    Parent or guardian,
    Teacher,
    Local authority,
    Government,
    Commerce and industry,
    The Church.
3. What, in your experience, is observable about the stages of development of a child and the way in which these changing needs are met by the education system?
4. To what extent is the potential development of a child extended or discouraged by the education system?
5. If a child is not taught, can he:
    Develop moral values?
    Learn to live in harmony with others?
    Know God's laws?
    Know God?

*

Tom would at times demonstrate the art of public speaking to a large assembly, showing how, with a simple gesture, a crowd could be controlled. For those who were interested there were his weekly speakers' groups. Similar groups met in Brussels, hosted by Paul Palmarozza, a specialist in computer-based education. 'Tom always praised and encouraged,' one member recalled.

Establishing contact with an audience was the first requirement. Gesture was a potent aid – and humour, if it was apt. It was important to project the voice. A firm opening was needed with not too many themes – three at most – illustrated by a story to give the various points immediacy. Then came consolidation, when proposals were confirmed from different points of view and grounded in experience. The conclusion needed to be uncomplicated, with a punch-line that was easy to remember.

Tom placed great importance on public speaking. It was in a way the engine of society. Good men and women needed to speak out and speak the truth. The Revd Basil Watson[4] went to the core of the matter:

Lots of people can talk: they have the gift of the gab and are entertaining. Others can read a script convincingly. But the real winners, the communicators, are those who, like Tom, can speak from the heart and stir others in the depth of their being by doing so.

*

Whether we like it or not, education is the responsibility of us all. We are all role models, especially a father and a mother. If society is sick, look to the family for the cause. Down the ages this has been a common call. It may not be the only cause but most would agree it is primary. Like father, like son.

The theme of family was prominent at Tom's conferences. To what examples and to what instruction are young minds subject? These questions are sobering. Modern pleasure-seeking ways can be neglectful of parental duty. The press highlights extreme examples: children roaming free at night, late enough to scrawl graffiti undetected, hardly speak of family discipline.

Education *is* primary. 'Jesus wept,' as the young Tom understood, because people had forgotten God. Today God's law is hardly being taught at all. Government directives are no substitute. To the 'have not' underclass they smack of 'them and us'.

CHAPTER 16

Europe

What we need is a 'Tom' in every country.
Henri Schoup

THE IDEA of a Brussels Conference grew out of a conversation between Tom Chapman and Margaret Bonstow while he still had his office in Church House. They had a good Brussels contact, Henri Schoup, a journalist of international repute who had worked for United Press, and was now a correspondent for the *New York Times* and the *Guardian* in London. It was Henri Schoup who in 1960 had broken the news of the Sharpville massacres in the township outside Johannesburg; he was ordered out of the country by the South African government the following day.

Tom and Margaret set off to meet Henri Schoup, arriving at last on the doorstep of a large neo-classical house in Brussels, plans to meet them at the airport having misfired. They were greeted by Verena van de Loo, who in her spare time was Henri's quadrilingual secretary.

'Tom looked like Father Christmas!' was Verena's first impression. From that moment grew their long friendship. In her delightful way, Henri's wife Joan takes up the story:

All I could think of to do was to take Tom around on a tourist-like trip of the city. Having exhausted the main sights and, wondering what to suggest next, I said, 'Would you like to see the English church?'

The church was in an attractive stone courtyard, tucked between the most prestigious shopping street, the Avenue Louise, and the equally elegant Boulevard des Arts. As luck would have it the minister had just come out of the church. Mystified by my introduction of Tom as liaison officer etc, etc, and mention of the Trade Union Movement (which Tom was instructing him about ...) I had a small inspiration and mentioned the Bishop of Leicester's connection with Tom's movement. It did help. Doors did open. 'A conference, an international conference?' he said. 'Well, would you like to hold it in the crypt?'

The crypt was unsuitable but the minister introduced them to his friend, Father Marie-Joseph Pudor, Abbot of the nearby Carmelite Monastery – a small, slight figure, radiating friendliness. He was wholly unassuming; Tom and he were instant friends. 'My monastery is yours,' the Abbot told him simply.

Joan Schoup continues:

Things moved astonishingly quickly after that and at a meeting of interested people Tom announced that Miss Verena van de Loo, whom Henri had loaned to smooth his linguistic way, was to be his organising secretary for Europe. What a strategist! Somehow Henri decided that such a *fait accompli* had to be accepted and what a gem Tom had annexed. Again what an amazingly fruitful and unexpected connection with the delightful Father Marie-Joseph of the monastery just down the road, who ended up reading the lesson in Westminster Abbey after one of Tom's London meetings, as did Verena herself. We truly believed and still do that Tom could move any old mountain that stood in his path if he believed it right.

But at that first conference in 1973 of the newly formed European Christian Industrial Movement (its initials in French spelt disarmingly MICE) we were all high on resolve and enthusiasm, let alone considerable faith that the linguistic tangle in Brussels would all get sorted out *in good time*.

At that first big meeting there was the kind of hope in the air that inspires – Flemish friends of ours were entirely charmed by Tom's true friendliness, with all his abiding faith. I had to remember that when he telephoned me from London before the event and said that he thought I should invite the British Ambassador and his wife to a small party to be held in *our house*, and organised by *me* – well, as a working journalist I had met many an odd situation, but nothing quite like this! For the life of me I could not think of any way to persuade the Ambassador that this was something he could not afford to miss. (That was Tom's view, of course.) I spoke to the Ambassador's lady who knew us vaguely as correspondents for newspapers and tried to clear up her total bafflement as to why anyone would want to organise something which was church, trade unions, faith and a bit of philosophy thrown in.[1] *Not* something diplomats generally feel moved to take part in.

Again, a voice spoke in my ear (we privately thought Tom had a hot line to the heavens) and it said, which I duly spoke forth to her ladyship: 'Well, we would much appreciate your presence here ... The Bishop of Leicester will come over, of course.'

'Leicester?' she said (it sounded rather Shakespearian), '*Leicester?* What's he doing over here? No one told us he was coming. Well, yes, I am sure we shall be able to attend.' And the ambassadorial party did arrive, which meant the police had to be involved, parking organised outside our home, armed policemen standing about, and the neighbours stunned by our sudden eminence.

It was a great party and Tom had a lovely time. He always did, of course. His was a truly great faith and he had the rare art of being able to communicate it to others. When it was all over and he was leaving, he told me we had a ghost in our attic. He was quite serious and I spent many hours in the next few years having a hunt for it.

Exorcising troubled spirits is of course a service that the Church provides. Tom knew all about that world.

Father Marie-Joseph's monastery was ideal. Now they had the venue and they had the chairs, but who would fill them? There was the London Group, of course, and others from the north of England: their numbers totalled thirty, maybe a few more. Then there were the Focolare, the 'little lights', members of a movement founded in Italy in response to the horrors of war – ordinary householders who vowed to live lives reflecting Christ's example.[2] Tom had already met some of these good people in London, and about fifty of them turned up for the conference. Then there were the local people, and some from France and Holland. The final total was substantial.

The Bishop of Leicester, Chairman of the Church of England's Board of Responsibility, presided, and through the good offices of Father Marie-Joseph the conference was addressed by the much respected Cardinal Suenens, a man noted for his forthright honesty. Tom's meeting with the Cardinal had echoes of his casual conversation with the Bishop's wife at Ripon College, Oxford. He was waiting in the Cardinal's ante-room when a man wearing a simple cassock came in and sat down beside him. They were soon deep in conversation. Tom assumed the man to be the Cardinal's secretary; it was only much later that he noticed his unmistakable ring. He had done it again!

The Conference was a great success. As the delegates went home the general feeling was one of having been uplifted. The task now was to keep the torch alight.

*

Hans Leewens, one of Tom Chapman's keen supporters, began to apply ECIM principles to his own company, van Ede and Partners – 'an authoritative voice in the world of Career Management, Outplacement and Coaching.'[3] He writes in forthright prose:

Christ, Plato and Ficino[4] are household names for consultants, staff and clients alike. Reflection and dialogue, a main feature of Tom's conferences, are practised by all. Again, love is a tangible asset in our houses and in all our dealings with our clients and with each other.

In the corporate world where management 'bonding' sessions can be physically tough, van Ede have a reputation for humanity and spirituality, but Hans Leewens is adamant van Ede is anything but soft. And they are a market leader.

Tom was invited to perform the ceremonial opening of van Ede's Hague branch office in May 1987 and was guest of honour at the celebration dinner. 'On both occasions', Hans writes, 'Tom was totally on top of the situation and made a great, and indeed an emotional impression on many people.' In the December 1987 edition of the *ECIM Newsletter*, Tom wrote, 'It must be a very rare privilege when one has the opportunity of seeing one's vision physically come true. Hans Leewens and his colleagues gave me that thrill ...'

It was Tom's words, spoken with sudden enthusiasm, which were to epitomise the van Ede company's aims. 'We need,' he had said, 'to foster the redistribution of talents in Europe.' When the company was formed, its slogan was 'Entrepreneuring with Talents'. The choice of Tom as guest of honour acknowledged him as their inspiration.

*

Tom Chapman's Paris venture in the mid seventies and his meeting with the French Federation of Christian Trade Unions 'appeared, as so many things with Tom, to have been a coincidence'. This was the view of Hans Leewens and the words capture the spirit of his brief Parisian visit.

It started with a lady arriving at the La Hulpe ECIM Conference to deliver a parcel: she met Tom and was captivated. On returning home she described the meeting to John Mansley, an Administrator at the Organisation for Economic Co-operation and Development (OECD) and a founder, as well as Chairman, of the OECD branch of the Union of International and European Christian Civil Servants (he went on to become International Chairman, covering areas such as Brussels, Strasbourg, Luxembourg, Florence and Geneva). On hearing about Tom, he immediately recognised the potential for a meeting of like minds. A national gathering of Christian trade unionist leaders in Paris was imminent and John Mansley saw to it that Tom was invited.

Hans Leewens met Tom at the airport; he remembers the plane being late. When they at last arrived at the meeting, the morning session was already over. Verena van de Loo, however, had already done a good job outlining the nature of the ECIM. 'She obviously touched them,' Hans recalled. When he and Tom arrived the twenty or so union leaders were descending the steps from their meeting place on their way to a nearby restaurant. At once they burst into spontaneous applause. Tom's entrance was perfect.

Tom spoke no French and his hosts little English; nevertheless they were at one in understanding. No doubt Verena helped greatly. The questions faced by the trade union leaders were ones on which Tom was expert. One concerned rule-book problems and a break-away faction. A second focused on post-Franco Spain and fears of a Communist take-over. Here

Tom was on safe territory, having coincidentally been to Spain not many months before.

No doubt Tom's input was both apt and timely, but in succeeding months and years contact lapsed. Although the French union leaders had generously offered the free use of their Paris premises for an ECIM event, no conference was arranged; the need had not arisen.

John Mansley, however, remained in touch — tenuously at first, his appointments diary rivalling that of a head of state; latterly he was a regular at Tom's Continental conferences. Tom Chapman and John Mansley had much in common, sharing a strong Christian commitment and courageous stance against the opposition they suffered. Both brought Christianity to the workplace.

A story related by John Mansley illustrates how, from small beginnings, men of good intent can achieve much. One warm day three OECD men, himself included, stopped for a beer after playing tennis. As usual on such occasions, the conversation was relaxed and easy. 'Why doesn't each of us donate 1% of his salary to a third-world project?' it was proposed and at once agreed. Other friends joined the project until soon the numbers were substantial. Thus was born the OECD War on Hunger Group. It had a budget approaching €74,000 in 2001. So simply begun, it ended up affecting thousands. A story right up Tom's street.

*

After Verena moved to England in 1984, the task of organising ECIM conferences and translating Tom's newsletters passed to Luc and Leen Glorie.[5] Most of the conferences were now held at Vogelzang, near Bruges. For Tom, in his late seventies and early eighties, they were demanding, but Luc and Leen's welcoming home in Brussels was a haven where he could recuperate and enjoy the lively company of the Glorie boys.

Luc observed that Tom exuded 'a glowing feeling of love. He was tolerant yet was very clear in what he wanted, and what he wanted was a European-wide Christian movement.' He also noticed that Tom guarded his independence, an independence that left him free to follow only Christ's teachings.

CHAPTER 17

The Cumbria Grand

There is a path which no fowl knoweth, and which the vulture's eye hath not seen.

Job 28:7

TOM CHAPMAN left his London home in September 1981 to set up house in Stainton, near Barrow, returning to his roots. He later developed diabetes and was unable to drive to London for his monthly group. The restriction was a blow but Tom's needs were met by Colin Smart, the publican of his local, who offered to drive him: this was not a one-off favour but a lasting commitment. Tom was a regular at both his Church and the pub – it is claimed that when he entered the latter all swearing stopped.

To those who received Tom's newsletters, superlatives such as 'the best conference ever', 'the most important conference ever' were familiar and, coming from Tom, somehow acceptable. Certainly there were few mediocraties in Tom's vision. Robert McNeill,[1] who helped Tom with conferences at the Cumbria Grand in these last years, makes the point that at them all 'the love was the same and always the best – an uplifting freshness'; as Hans Leewens adds emphatically, 'It was the love of a just man.'

Robert McNeill recalls Tom's sparkling vivacity in the cut and thrust of evening carpet sessions. Pat was as ever an enormous help, he emphasises, working quietly behind the scenes, never making a fuss. Tom was very grateful. His friends, Albert and Audrey Sandbank, Ron Heaps and of course Robert and Verena Watson, were also always there to lend support, but Tom was no frail old man surrounded by a sentimental glow (he would have hated that). Although he no longer had physical strength his inner vigour was almost tangible.

Tom was never perfect and would have been first in the queue to pronounce it: with his surging emotions he could turn maverick. When his vision was thwarted by pessimists, or even by the justly cautious, he could be difficult. But his generous spirit invariably prevailed.

There were many callers at his home in Stainton, including a young couple, Andrew and Delyth Cresswell,[2] who were both very fond of Tom. Andrew writes:

Tom's generosity and hospitality were boundless. Pat and Tom were always 'at home' to visitors and would always insist on taking us out for dinner whenever we called in. He was interested in everyone he came into contact with and wanted to know about their families, their work and their concerns. He wanted to help. He was inspiring, energetic, engaged, motivated, committed and an extraordinary person to know. Delyth and I feel privileged to have had the opportunity to enjoy his company many times during his last ten years.

Tom's London visits were dear to him but the Cumbria Grand conferences, being local to Stainton, naturally became the focus of his evening years. They were times of reunion with old friends, of renewal in good company, and times for spiritual reflection. They were also more than that, much more. Tom had grown inwardly, or rather the trappings of a vigorous life had fallen away to reveal, with growing clarity, a quiet and compelling presence.

The Cumbria Grand Hotel, a rambling Victorian building with shades of grandeur, was perfect for Tom's purpose, and there was ample space for young people. Indeed it was to the young that Tom was turning more and more, and they were listening. This was not polite parent-driven deference to an old man, it was how it was.

Love remained Tom's constant theme. 'Love has no bounds,' he said. 'There is nowhere it can stop. The very reason for our groups existing is to practice in the art of giving love.'[3] But he welcomed humour. It punctured self-importance. Pat once left a card by his computer and he immediately included its words in the August 2000 *Newsletter*: 'I wanted to go out and change the world, but I couldn't find a babysitter.'

Tom's youthful resolve, if examined superficially, could be dismissed as utterly naive. Such commitments usually collapse in weeks, like one's own New Year resolutions. Clearly Tom's resolve was in a wholly different class. His constancy throughout the years shows that he had tapped in at a much deeper level.

*

From the beginning the ECIM had been blessed with influential and supportive presidents and patrons, men of broad experience and understanding. The first President, the Rt Revd Ronald Williams, Bishop of Leicester, appreciated Tom's sincerity and supported him unfailingly, first when Tom was at Church House and later when the ECIM was formed.

This continuity of support was invaluable at the difficult time of transition; it preserved the vital link with the Church.

The second President, the Rt Revd Ross Hook, MC, Bishop of Bradford and the Archbishop of Canterbury's Chief of Staff between 1980 and 1984, had been a naval man seconded to the Marines as Chaplain during the Second World War. He had served with Fitzroy Maclean in Yugoslavia – not a chaplaincy for the timid!

The current Patron of the ECIM, the Revd Basil Watson, OBE, was Chaplain to the Fleet Air Arm during the war and first met Ross Hook at Bari in southern Italy. Bari was a staging post for activities in Yugoslavia. They came to know each other well. The Revd Watson described his friend as 'very much the soldier in the field' and they approached the ECIM by different routes, Ross Hook through the Church and Basil Watson by way of the City, for after the war he became Vicar of St Lawrence Jewry, the church of the Corporation of the City of London.

There is a humorous story about his appointment. St Lawrence Jewry being at the centre of City life, the vacancy attracted nearly a hundred applicants, eight eventually being selected for interview by some twenty Aldermen and Common Councillors. At St Lawrence Jewry there was no parish life as such – apart from in the Barbican, there are few residents – even fewer at weekends. At his interview Basil Watson was direct, 'There is unlikely to be a mothers' union or a Sunday school. What else could a naval chaplain want? It is money for old rope!' The reaction of the rather humourless Chairman was: 'Do you want the job?' but other members of the panel burst out laughing. When the Lord Mayor's secretary, a retired admiral, was telephoned his response was brusque: 'A naval chaplain without a sense of humour would be worse than useless and a Vicar of St Lawrence Jewry without a sense of humour would be worse than useless too!' Basil Watson was chosen for the job.

Afterwards he invited the retired admiral, who had served as a close aide to Lord Mountbatten, for a gin, the traditional way of expressing gratitude. 'I was thanking the Admiral', he said, 'whose quip undoubtedly got me the job.' The Revd Watson held the post for sixteen years.

Although familiar Church routine was absent at St Lawrence Jewry, the new appointee was by no means idle. His Wednesday Platform, a weekly lunchtime talk kept strictly to the City lunch break, drew an impressive array of speakers including future Prime Minister Margaret Thatcher, and was regularly reported in the press.[4]

After the Rt Revd Ross Hook's ECIM Presidency, Tom faced a

dilemma: he had his sights set on two men but there could be only one President. The idea of having patrons solved the problem for him. The Revd Bill Gowland, Principal of Luton Industrial College, and the Revd Basil Watson became joint Patrons.

The Revd Gowland, President of the 1979-80 Methodist Conference, was a very old and trusted friend of Tom's. They were on the same wavelength; respect was mutual. Being the youngest son of a farm labourer, Bill Gowland, like Tom, had been well acquainted with poverty in his early years. 'From his parents', his obituary reads, 'he learned about Christianity, thrift and hard work [and] always regarded a sixteen-hour day as normal.'[5] His early hardships were never forgotten; he was firmly committed to the belief that the Gospel should be taken to where people 'work, toil and sweat and swear'[6] It is little wonder that he and Tom were close. Sadly he passed away suddenly in 1991, leaving the Revd Watson as sole Patron.

Like all the presidents and patrons, Basil Watson became a regular at Tom's conferences and monthly Church House meetings. His easy manner made him popular with ECIM members. For his part he found 'a happy team' surrounding Tom, 'always one together'.

*

Trustees are often dim figures in the background called upon to dig into their coffers at times of trouble. ECIM trustees, however, were never so shadowy. They were active participants, regular attendees at conferences and meetings and hands-on occasions such as the Barrow strike. An early trustee who acted as treasurer was John L. Stevenson, a member of the City of London Common Council and of the Gardeners Company. It was through John Stevenson that Tom was made a Freeman of the City.

Jack Peel was another early trustee. Roger Pincham pays the following tribute to him:

Like Tom, Jack had a hands-on industrial background, including driving steam engines. As a full-time trades unionist he rose to become General Secretary of the Union of Dyers, Bleachers and Textile Workers from 1966-73 and served on the General Council of the TUC from 1966-1972. Those were the years of Barbara Castle's 'In place of strife' initiative and the Industrial Relations Act which led to the defeat of Harold Wilson's Government in 1970. Almost alone amongst prominent TUC leaders, Jack supported the Castle line and liked to use the phrase 'militant moderation' to describe the new unifying factor which he believed essential to mobilise the positive forces in society and outflank the forces of destruction. Jack was also a strong pro-European and was nominated by Edward Heath to become Director of Industrial Relations in the Social Affairs Directorate when Britain joined the EEC in 1973. He held that appointment until 1979. Jack Peel was also on the Industrial Committee of the Church of England Board of Social Responsibility. With his wide experience, shared objectives and high public profile he remained an invaluable and unswerving supporter during his years in Brussels. Throughout he had the staunch support of his wife Barbara. Jack continued to attend conferences and do all he could even after being overtaken by ill health, which led to his premature death in 1993. Tom had lost one of his closest friends and it was a cruel blow for the ECIM.

James Armstrong,[7] the current Chairman of the Trustees of ECIM, and Peter Green[8] were there from the beginning and were part of what the Revd Watson called Tom's 'happy team'. Peter Green remembers the inaugural meeting held in the Robing Room of the House of Lords, undoubtedly hosted by the Lord Bishop of Leicester.

In Tom's final years two new trustees were incorporated, Iain Cairncross[9] and Ian Mason.[10] Both had known Tom for a long time and both had spoken at conferences. Ian Mason was a regular at Tom's speakers' groups in the seventies. 'I learnt more about speaking from Tom,' he said, 'than I did at Bar School!' Iain Cairncross hails from the North and lives quite close to Tom's last home at Stainton, so he was on hand to visit frequently and help Tom arrange his Grange-over-Sands conferences.

CHAPTER 18

The Trip to Moscow

... What doth the Lord require of thee, but to do justly, and to love mercy and to walk humbly with thy God?

Micha 6:8

At the height of his powers Tom Chapman stood four-square against the Communist threat. At the age of 79 he was given the chance to visit Moscow at the invitation of his friend Bill Finley. Bill recalls how thrilled Tom was: here was a golden opportunity to spread the word, to speak of Christianity. 'The students loved him,' Bill recalls, 'and when he left they called the room where he had conducted his informal "carpet" sessions, "Tom's Room".'

The visit, from 6th to 13th April 1993, was reported in Tom's diary:

6th: Drove slowly from Stainton to Albert's in five hours. Had supper with Albert, Audrey, Verena and Bob and, of course, Ron.* They are five people who are as vivacious now as they were twenty-five years ago – little knowing that this company and our surroundings would be in such deep contrast to the world I was to be in for the next five days. The vision must remain in the background of this report as the datum line.

7th. Driven to the airport by Albert and Audrey, where I met Bill Finley of Bill Finley Associates who has entirely sponsored my visit to Moscow. Bill took over all arrangements and expertly continued to do so until I returned to England. The journey to Moscow was quite good and we duly arrived in time. We were greeted by the Director and Deputy Director of the Moscow International Business School which is part of the Russian Economic Academy, which I understand is the largest and most famous in Russia. It was built in 1907 and has remained operational throughout all national changes.

My first impressions were not good. There was the gloom of dusk turning to darkness, without the welcoming lights the stranger might expect. Everything is too reminiscent of the wartime blackout. But everyone we met was most kind and friendly, making me feel ungrateful for the initial shock.

8th The expected accommodation did not materialise, nor was any explanation offered. Should I accept the students' quarters or insist on being shown to a hotel?

---

*Albert and Audrey Sandbank, Bob and Verena Watson and the late Ronald Heaps.

The decision was mine and I felt the mission ahead of me was becoming more and more obvious each moment; I have a natural talent for communication that might be of use to these young people, so I accepted the students' quarters. The students soon became my friends and by subtle negotiation I had my own bath and toilet.

The next day began with a long, painful walk to the restaurant, accompanied by Bill and a lady interpreter. The others had already eaten so only I had breakfast. Indeed I was the only customer each morning. The interpreter, Elena Zubkova, Head of Foreign Relations, was a splendid conversationalist and impressed me with her knowledge of the Moscow Academy of which the International Business School is a small part. Her description of the Russian people was interesting – there is no middle class; everyone is either very rich or very poor. Elena, whose husband I had met the night before, is a civil servant – obviously very rich!

Elena told me, without my asking, that she is a Communist and an atheist. This I recognised as inevitable, though her charm and enthusiastic assistance to me later proved her to be a loyal, brilliant teacher and I was most impressed by the quality of the students she taught.

There was a mile-long walk to the Academy along an uneven road. The many water-filled potholes were quite grim. The cost of repairs must, in my opinion, be very much less than the damage to transport as well as the inconvenience to pedestrians. Ahead of us was the Academy – a number of typical academy buildings, all painted battleship grey. They could have been made to look much more attractive.

If that sounds like criticism, it becomes almost astounding in contrast to the smiling, happy faces I met on arrival. Frankly I was amazed at the cheerfulness of the students in the hallways and staircases. Few were well dressed. The tutors were obvious. Most students were smoking, except in class. Then I met the students in the Business Academy, clearly different – all well dressed in comparison with those in the corridors. It was made clear to me that these were the children of the wealthy. They were the elite. The tutors and students here all spoke good English and most politely gave me the first opportunity of an impromptu 'carpet session', whilst Bill was attending to other business. This proved to be a useful publicity exercise for me later.

Bill arrived with Mikhail Popov and we set off by car to what I was told would be a Russian Church Hall in 'down town' Moscow. Our driver for the week was a university trained architect. This was my first glimpse of Moscow in daylight.

We arrived at a very, very run-down area. The poverty was as bad as any I have seen on television or film. The poor are very poor. Here we were introduced to a Russian layman of the Russian Orthodox Church. One of his duties was to find the wherewithal to feed five hundred homeless people every day. We joined in a meal for the homeless and had a bowl of celery soup followed by a plate of green beans – most nourishing.

Alexander Ogorodnikov is Chairman of the Christian Democratic Union of Russia and also Chief Editor of the Christian Democracy Messenger. He was also active, he told me, in the Ecology movement in Moscow. He later showed us around the warehouse below and introduced us to his five lady assistants and then came his 'sales talk'. This movement owned one floor of a large and famous building on the other side of Moscow and all he needed was ten thousand pounds to buy the whole building. The objective was to found an International Open University there. At the end of the seventeenth century Peter the Great, then a boy, first dreamed of the great Russian fleet in this building and much later Napoleon slept there. A.O. was to be one of the speakers at the next day's seminar. I doubt if we will be buying the building!

9th: This was the day of the seminar and the introduction of the 'Holistic Movement' Bill and Mikhail had in mind. There were to be five speakers. The hall was an amphitheatre and the acoustics were splendid. The hall was packed with eager young faces of both sexes – to me a wonderful opportunity beyond my wildest dreams to spell out a message to souls.

Elena, the Principal of the School, introduced Bill. I cannot do justice to the subject he introduced. I can best describe it as something like my own idea of ecumenism plus, in his view, a compromise including humanism, politics and any other altruistic or alternative religion.

I was not invited to embrace Bill's concept of belief. My contribution to the seminar was, as I saw it, to give an account of my life's ideals, how they came about and how far I had reached, and to offer a glimpse of the obstacles en route. By now you will know this story as well as I do, but it is important that I bore you once more for the purpose of reading the minds that were behind the questions – which were soon prolific.

I followed Bill, with the Principal as my interpreter. I think we were a good team. I began by thanking my audience for the privilege of addressing them. What had we in common? – Tom Chapman, seventy years ago and they now – in a world in the same state of decline and apparent despair. We each had the same burning desire to put the world to rights, as I had had seventy years ago. The same fire is burning today – the differences being the restrictions and limited imagination. My world all those years ago stretched from Barrow to Ulverston, but now, thanks to them, it stretched to Moscow. We belong to the same ancient family which goes back as far as Adam. At least that cannot be biologically challenged once we accept that we share the same problems and the desire to put the world to rights. And if we persuade others to do likewise, change is just around the corner.

The example that fills me with hope is that the scene I saw on the path in Moscow is so typical of what I might see in any enlightened country in the world. Walking along the path in fours were about forty young children, full of life and every six rows or so was a young teacher, each like a hen with her chicks. It was a beautiful picture of renewed hope and inspiration. Those children are as much my moral responsibility as anyone in this hall. Together our vision encompasses the world. We have advanced much since I first set about putting the world right! Your task is not easier though the tools for the work improve. Every one of you is better educated than I was or am now. Communications and transport have removed more of the difficulties as well as increasing them in other directions. Radio, television, the telephone were either unknown or unavailable to me when I had to choose to believe in a God or not. Thank God I chose to believe. It was the instinct that gave rise to the vision of the future and the vision gave me hope.

I spoke a little too long and there was little time for the questions. We were told I would be speaking again.

Question: Why do you worship idols and icons? Do you need gold crosses to pray to? Why do you have so many icons around the walls? Do you worship all of them?

Answer: I worship none of them. Before I entered this room I said a prayer. I needed no cross to guide me. Some people see icons as guides to prayer but certainly not as Gods in themselves.

Question: If a company has one hundred and ninety-nine who steal from the one, are they all thieves?

Answer: If the one still has a profit after the stealing, then who is the thief?

There were variations of the same questions, with obvious answers. I felt that I had the sympathy of my audience. No questions were hostile. The seminar closed for lunch.

The speakers for the afternoon session were, without exception, openly political and though my interpreter did her best, and sought assistance with a young student to change the tone, I was as bored as the audience who were at least able to simply walk out. This they did spasmodically until only six were left. For me it should have been interesting to hear different views but all that I learnt was that politics are the same the world over and the 'blarney' differed little.

I have all the speeches in Russian – as useful as if they were Chinese! The one splendid moment for me was when, walking with others from the Academy, a young man stopped and, shaking hands, asked: 'What can we do now!' Before I could reply to this question of a lifetime, a voice over my shoulder said: 'Mr Chapman will answer later.' My response was to add, 'This I solemnly promise.'

We spent the evening at the Kremlin Palace of Conferences where we saw the ballet *Cinderella*. It was magnificent. Returning, two or three came for a 'carpet session', along with the interpreters who were there as guests. I enjoyed it.

10th: Bill Finley's clubs I would call 'groups'. Their purpose was to learn how to address an audience. About fifty or so met in the Academy, some with their girl-friends. All were bilingual and clearly interested. Bill began by explaining once again his theory of Holistic Development.[1] I was not involved. There followed reports from the various clubs.

I was then asked to give a demonstration of public speaking. To my amazement it is easier than would at first appear. 'Body language' is universal. It was, if anything, easier than teaching an English group. I enjoyed myself and felt my audience shared my pleasure. This now gave me the opportunity to answer my young friend's question, so vital to the whole expedition: 'What can I do?' I told my audience of the pleasure the question gave me and that I could see before me the double of the Tom Chapman of sixty years before. The Mission of 'putting the world to rights' was not only by example in truth and reliability, though both are essential, but also in making sure the sound from the lips is of love. Once a sound leaves my lips it is in the atmosphere and I cannot take it back. That is the greatest need of the whole world today, as it was when I began my mission – to fill the atmosphere with sounds of love of such power and quality that it will overcome the stench of evil, hatred and greed – the negative force which is all too easily mixed with squalor, filth and

THE TRIP TO MOSCOW   81

dirt and which can be seen by the eyes and removed with water and a good stiff brush!

The questions were the best I have had for many years. I wish I had time to quote them all. 'Why should I bother living?' and 'Where do you get your vision from?'

Answer: I believe that each one of us has an individual vision between God and oneself. The vision forms during the period in our mother's womb: What are we going to do outside? As we grow, though, we meet the strange world as it is. We tend to forego the vision for the reality we meet and, unfortunately, find the reality easier to accept. The vision in the womb was the perfect one. This we will learn for ourselves some day.

At the moment I have the honour of addressing the potential leaders of the largest single group of people in the ancient family, other perhaps than the Chinese and it is at the moment in time when the need is greatest to spread the word of Love in the atmosphere. This is your greatest role. It can begin in this very room and spread throughout the world. That is your vision and becomes more vivid when we remember the children I saw on the street in Moscow yesterday.

Question: Why should I not eat my enemy if I hate him?

Answer: Apart from unnecessary indigestion, if you remove the hate and replace it with love – and it may not be easy – history has proved that the man you are now loving becomes a friend. No war has ever achieved a moral victory for anyone. (Variations, some more profound than others, none frivolous.)

11th: Attended the Moscow Protestant Chaplaincy for Easter Communion. It is a wonderful church, next to the KGB headquarters. The church was packed and I heard the most beautiful singing I have probably ever heard in my life. The world-famous Moscow Chamber Choir sang Gretchaninov.[2]

Later, after sightseeing, I had lunch with Bill's secretary's mother and family at their home – a lovely experience. In the evening we had another 'carpet session at home which I enjoyed as much as everyone else.

12th: Sightseeing most of the day. I visited my first Russian hotel! Then goodbyes to so many new friends.

13th: Returned to London, Audrey and Albert and supper later with them and Verena and Bob, Luc Leen and the boys. If I have left behind that same Love, the supper party replenished it and every second of pain from this arthritis was worthwhile.

Tom now had friends in the city of the fallen regime he had fought so long. A bridge had been built.

CHAPTER 19

Unity

The love is from God; and of God, and towards God.

Words spoken by a man of the desert and
recorded by Lawrence of Arabia[1]

I WAS PRIVILEGED to enjoy a brief interview with Tom before he was due to address a meeting at St James School near Olympia in London in September 2000.

Some of my impressions were noted at that time: Tom was frail in body and he was supported by friends into the school's reception. Gratefully he sat down. Tea was produced and we were left alone with no one interrupting. So the questions began. Tom had no wait-until-I-settle reservations. His responses were at once open and gentle in quality, a sharing with a friend.

After a long walk to the meeting room, the questions continued. Were they tiring? 'No,' he answered. This was the truth, not polite posturing. Suddenly it was obvious: words came; he wasn't in the least disturbed.

'What do they want me to say?' he asked before the meeting started. On the surface understandable concerns briefly spun, but beneath there was certainty. There was no doubt that he would speak effectively; it was sensed that he was resting in the substance, love, that he kept charging us to seek, and it was from this substance, love, that he spoke with fearless simplicity.

This profound simplicity is evident from a conversation, reported in the August 2001 *ECIM Newsletter*, between Tom Chapman and Verena Watson, conducted at Tom's bedside in Cumbria.

Life is so simple and so beautiful. Love makes the bird fly and the flower grow. Love moves the clouds in the sky and makes the leaf drop from the tree. Love shows in the need and in the exact fulfilment of the need. All we have to do is just do what is there to be done, whatever there is. Every action is God's plan, every gesture is important. Every cell is important. Every single person is important in God's plan.

Can one see love? Of course you can!
Can you hear love? Yes! It is all the sounds.
Can you taste love? Yes!

Can you think love? *Of course!* Thought is naturally *love*. You have to work hard to make it other.

That is our job, to tell people about love, to persuade people to love. Then they will be happy. God wants us to be happy. We only need to love.

Everything is love. Everything changes. Everything is new all the time. What you see, God made yesterday. But love is always there. That is what everything is made of. That is God Himself.

Tom passed away on 29th October 2001 and the funeral was held at Ulverston Parish Church on 7th November.

CHAPTER 20

The Need Remains

The Principles of true politics are those of morality enlarged.

Edmund Burke[1]

How quickly we forget, yet how quickly memory is rekindled. A brief visit to a newspaper library and the strike-infested culture of a generation past seems to be reborn. *The Times* of 30th October 1970 has a photograph of a man walking down a path flanked by head-high heaps of bagged-up rubbish – the site is Berkley Square. That was the Council Strike.

Have we left all this behind? No prudent man would dare to answer yes. The Marxist cult is still abroad but now it has a different wardrobe, fire-proofed with political correctness. Then there is the rigid Right, feeding on the people's fears and on their sense of being ignored.

Somewhere in the middle is common sense. Birds need both wings to fly. True, they have a right wing and a left, but a bird that uses only one wing circles, if it flies at all. There are perplexing problems. One is the ownership of property which separates the haves from the have-nots. During recent decades this fissure had grown to a chasm. Yet the lottery of ownership is seen to be a valid perk and the crushing burden placed on first-time buyers, if they can afford the mortgage, is regretted sadly as a fact of life. Is this God's law or man's forgetfulness? Clearly there are enormous questions for those who seek the rule of reason, the full expression of God's love. The questions are pressing: if good men fail to act, hate-filled protest will.

So what should we do? Communism failed. Capitalism is not too healthy either. What is the answer? If Tom were back with us in the vigour of his youth, where would he stand? Surely he would stand where bridges could be built, where the power of love could hold men to a common purpose. If man could keep the great commandment to love his neighbour as himself there would be no problem.[2] Such is the power of love: 'The only power,' as Tom said, 'that can defeat hate.' Such love would be at one with justice for love without justice is not love at all,

84

while justice without love is little more than vengeance. This is why for Tom love was never sentimental: the ideal and the practical are not separate, one informs the other and ever-present need unites them. God's love is for the workplace through the week, not only for the altar rail on Sunday. Rendering unto Caesar what belongs to Caesar does not mean that God can be ignored.

This is an area where all who are of good intent can work, and for those in management or those who have a role in union leadership there is a wider opportunity. But men like Tom are special, for when their open hearts receive the call there is no question of them not obeying. Their path is hard and takes enormous courage. Even so their faith remains rock-firm despite circling troubles.

A striking experience of Sergei Tarassenko echoes this:

> I do not know whether you have ever seen a cyclone. I was a pilot in the French Air Force and I remember flying only once in my life through one. It is very dangerous over a cyclone. But in the midst of it there is the eye of the cyclone and there is complete silence there. Do you know why? It is not because there is a vacuum or emptiness. It is just because it is the centre where all the forces are in perfect equilibrium. There is a perfect equilibrium of all the forces, and this is why there is silence. This is where God speaks to us, because Jesus does not stand somewhere at a distance or in a remote place. Jesus speaks to us from the midst of the storm, from that place of silence and equilibrium, and he speaks to us through His Word.[3]

We, as human beings, have this choice: to hold to the silent centre or to swing out, wild and frantic, with the storm. It is at the silent centre that the open heart will hear that still small voice. That was what Tom trusted. The swirling clouds may be wonderful to watch but it's where we're watching from that counts.

*In Memory
of
Margaret Bonstow*

All who attended the conferences of the sixties and seventies will remember the vivacity and omnipresence of Margaret. Her job as Tom's Secretary/Assistant was a true vocation. Nothing was too much trouble. Yet she was always very much herself and unafraid of stating her opinion.

Margaret was Tom's Secretary 1961-c.1979

List of Appendices

A	The Personnel Manager and the Do's and Don'ts of Bargaining: Tom Chapman, c.1980	89
B	Portrait of a Movement: Tom Chapman describes the picture	97
C	The Bridgebuilders: Notes on a talk by James Armstrong, OBE, FREng, Chairman of the Trustees of the ECIM, January 1972	99
D	Our Common Future: Conference address by Roger Pincham, CBE, 27th December 1989	103
E	Divinity Shines in Every Heart: Closing speech by Tom Chapman, Wadderton Conference, Blackwell, 30th March 1969	105
F	Our Common Future: Peter G. Green, BSc (EstMan), FRICS, ECIM Trustee, c.1990	107
G	Scargill, 21st January 1973: Extract from a speech by Dr Sergi Tarassenko	111
H	Westminster Conference, 1975: Extracts from speeches	113
I	Common Cause: Hugh Lunghi	115
J	Love and Truth: Towards the Millennium, ECIM Grange-over-Sands Conference, 1996	116
K	Extracts from *ECIM Newsletters*: Tom Chapman, 1998-2001	117

Appendices

APPENDIX A

The Personnel Manager and the Do's and Don'ts of Bargaining
Tom Chapman, c.1980

It must be clearly understood that there are always two sides to every conflict in negotiations. A bargain is not a bargain unless it is agreed willingly or unwillingly by both sides. Nevertheless, it is also true that both sides have a common objective. Basically, this common objective is the continued success or prosperity of the company, the industry, or even the nation involved. Furthermore, the role of the Christian is precisely the same on either side. The difficulties vary only in degree, for there can be no clearly defined Christian policy as such relating to any overall problem. It is always for each Christian, whether he be on one side or the other, to relate each problem, however great or small, to the great commandments. The teachings of Our Lord Jesus have no separate instructions for management or employee or trade unionist. Each in his bargaining position has the same two commandments to which he may relate his problem (*St Mark* 12:30-1).

The negotiator or bargainer representing the employer is normally referred to as 'Management', and the person speaking on behalf of that management at the first point in all discussions is known as the Personnel Manager. The role of the Personnel Manager has never been clearly defined, for his task of keeping good relations between management and ordinary workpeople is rarely defined, and still more rarely understood. The man who has this task is in a unique position. When he sits at the table opposite the men's representatives, he represents the management. And then later when he sits at the table facing his superiors, the management, he represents the men. But his own personal advancement depends upon the management who pay his salary, and not upon the men. It is a successful management, who, understanding the importance of industrial peace, listens attentively to the Personnel Manager pleading the case of the men, and are not offended and do not regard him as a traitor, even though they may not agree with what he says. Rarely do they have industrial unrest in their factories.

The position of Personnel Manager is not unlike that of an architect. An architect has obligations towards the owner of a site, and also on the other hand to the building contractors. To the contractors he represents the owner, and to the owner he represents the contractors. Whilst this relationship is held in balance, work proceeds apace. When the balance is seriously disturbed, work can be brought to a standstill. In the course of my experience over many years now, well over half of the unofficial strikes would never have arisen had management listened to their own representative and become aware of the problems of industrial relationships. One of the greatest needs of the Church in this field of industrial relations is to understand and further the mutual trust, which in the economic field is a condition of our very existence as a nation. The great British institutions which today remain cornerstones of world trade were founded, quite literally, upon a handshake as a pledge of goodwill. The merchants and sea captains who met in the coffee houses in the City of London to make their bargains laid the foundations of a trading system which has rarely been equalled. Indeed, this unique trust has made London the centre that it is.

But before the proposition mentioned above is carried too far, we have to remember that the merchants who made their bargains in those days met as equals. By no stretch of the imagination could it be said that management and labour meet as equals today, nor have they done so for several hundred years. It is an instinctive understanding of this weakness that makes organised labour so prone to intransigence on questions such as wages and redundancy, and discipline of human behaviour, particularly on the factory floor. Since the war, in many large firms with good personnel management, respect and recognition of human dignity have increased considerably. It is, however, still a burning issue in many factories throughout the land that a man who may have worked on the factory floor for forty years cannot be trusted to walk in at the commencement of the day, yet his daughter, who may be eighteen years of age, employed as a junior typist on staff, is trusted to walk in and out as she may please. This one well-known anomaly is typical of many of the hundreds of problems that are the affair of the Personnel Manager.

A Personnel Officer in one firm may be a kind of junior clerk. In another firm, for example in the majority of the car industry, he may be a Director with a seat on the Board and a real say in the firm's policy. In general practice he may occupy any of a hundred points in between these two extremes. In the course of my lifetime, I suppose I have met almost every type of Personnel Officer or Manager or Director that one could meet, and in all cases their success was dependant less upon their knowledge than upon their wisdom and the ability to reach hearts and understand other people's hearts. The size and complexity of so many of our industrial undertakings has largely obliterated the age-old relationship of a master craftsman and his men. The head of a big business nowadays is usually less a craftsman in terms of a product than in administrative, financial and marketing techniques. In large firms, the business of the human side of management has become increasingly delegated to specialists. In smaller firms, a good Works Manager does not need a personnel assistant. I well remember negotiating the price for a particular job, when the Personnel Manager, whom I had known all my life, offered to take off his coat and do the job himself. He was able to call our bluff because we knew as well as he did that he was quite capable of tackling the job and doing it in the time that we were asking.

But, broadly, the work of a Personnel Department, whether this is handled by a separate section or the responsibility of the Works Manager or the Company Secretary, is based on five important functions. These are: employment, education and training, working conditions, industrial relations, and what I would call pastoral services that cannot be defined by any agreement and must always be based on the need of the moment. For the performance of all these functions, close contact is necessary with both top management and supervisory staff lower down the lines, for two reasons: to carry out the instructions stemming from management policy, and at the same time to feed back important, vital information which may shape that policy. It is a foolish Managing Director who ignores information coming back from the factory floor.

The five functions I have mentioned cover an immense field, and whilst in latter years Government have taken some of the responsibility, the functions themselves are very rarely covered to their full extent even now in any one firm. Personnel management is the Cinderella of a firm because it shows apparent non-productivity on the accounts sheets, but the wisest of managements know that a very good Personnel Department with a close relationship with a very good Convenor and Shop Stewards – these will be discussed later – saves any firm millions of pounds every year of its life.

FUNCTIONS

Under the heading of Employment, the selection of workers is a big subject on its own. There is a considerable bibliography on the relative merits of various methods of selection, from the hiring of the casual hand on the spot to the mystique of psychological tests for personality and manual dexterity. The psychological tests are still a mystery to me, and I feel sure to the majority of really good Personnel Managers throughout the land. Again, for the best possible use to be made of available workforce, it is necessary for progress records to be kept, with a view to transfer or promotion; and then the good Personnel Manager keeps his eye on the aging workers, who may need less exacting work to be found for them. Job evaluation and payment of piece rates may be such a huge task that this is mainly done now by computer. Whilst education and training facilities vary greatly from one firm to another, there is no reason whatsoever for a firm to neglect such facilities, for the Government, indeed the Factory Acts, now lay down compulsory requirements for the training of the young worker. We can feel proud in the United Kingdom of the training and education facilities offered. The Personnel Department is also responsible for the maintenance of good working conditions, for which the Factory Act lays down minimum requirements and welfare services which often overlap. Safety regulations, special clothing, canteens, recreational facilities, help with transport and housing, are only a few of the vast number of matters dealt with in the Personnel Office.

Each firm, whether it be large or small, has its own way of life, its own atmosphere. This is compounded of many different particles, each in its own right significant. Outwardly it may appear to be dominated by its mechanical process, the whir of machines or the noise of the typewriters, or the flash of the welding rod, the hiss of the molten metal, the ingrained smell that is so personal to one particular community, within and outside the gates. I have never known any successful firm which did not have its own life and its own team spirit. That's the success of a good Personnel Director.

In towns which are dominated by one industry, the influence of the firm and its policy in human relations are marked and powerful. There is, of course, Barrow-in-Furness. Vickers was Barrow-in-Furness. Pilkintons is, and has been for very many years, St Helens. There must be no conflict between the way of life in the factory and the home. No man should be asked to live to two sets of principles, of honesty and fair-dealing at home, the devil take the hindmost at work; at home the head of a household, at work the statistical digit, too often recognised by number rather than by name. It is because of this maladjustment between industry and society that it has been possible for an industrial consultant to say that business still looks on its employees as economic men, seeking exclusively economic objectives, whereas in reality social objectives are more important to most employees. *Esprit de corps* is as important in any factory as a good lighting system or ventilation system. Both serve a similar function, one psychological and the other material, but neither is more important than the other.

UNOFFICIAL STOPPAGES

In the field of industrial relations – I personally prefer to call it human relations – it is the Personnel Officer whom the local officials first seek out when the Shop Steward or Convenor reports a dispute that cannot be settled on the spot. Unnecessary industrial disputes are rarely due to the worker alone. It is usually in the first instance fifty-fifty, a personal affront or misunderstanding. If management understood human relations, the majority of unofficial stoppages would never take place. A good Personnel Manager knows this, and so does a good factory Trade Union convenor. Management is outwitted by men of no great education or advantage in life should the Personnel Manager lose his temper. Such a man is unworthy of holding his job. It is equally true that one can accidentally use a sentence which may be picked up by an evil man on one side or the other, and cause an unofficial strike. Many years ago, a particular firm decided in all fairness to give the men in their employ notice of impending redundancy, and this was of course done by the Personnel Manager addressing the whole of the stewards. The shop stewards were not reasonable; they reacted strongly and indignantly demanded, 'What do you mean by redundancy? Is it really necessary?' The Personnel Officer, having considered that he had given a fair warning long before it had been necessary, was naturally angry, but he had forgotten that this was something that a Personnel Manager must never do. He said in his anger, 'Thirteen men could go at once, this very moment. We don't need them.' This was a foolish statement to make because it was not the original intention of management to make anyone redundant immediately. It led to a strike, which was exactly what the wildcat, strike-mad shop stewards wanted, and from that strike that particular firm did not recover. It literally went bankrupt.

The man who has the whip-hand must never lose his temper. He can afford to be patient. But it is also a fact that you must not lose your temper if you are at a disadvantage in a situation. To do so is always not only dangerous but an absolutely stupid thing to do. However, as long as managements regard the workers as enemies to be made to work for as long as possible for as little as possible, then one can expect endless trouble. All my working life I have heard it said by foolish management, when twelve men are queuing up for one man's job, 'We can deal with Trade Unions.' Nothing can be more untrue in the economic structure that man is weaving whether he likes it or not, in the new pattern of progress. Under economic pressure, in the last century the workers starved; in the next century all will starve. Aggressiveness almost always hides fear, and this is as true of management as it is of the factory floor. The solidarity of the workers or trade unionists in industrial action can be terrifying; the tension engendered is hair-raising. One can sense the electric atmosphere when one enters the office of a Personnel Manager who is afraid of strike action taking place. It takes a strong man to stand unmoved in this situation. But the fact remains that the Manager who knows his men also knows their needs. A smile is far better than a frown, and dignity is not necessarily to order a man to stand up, but dignity more often means saying with a grin on your face, 'Come on, let's sit down and talk it over.' By far the majority of Personnel men over the age of forty are competent, and are capable of holding their own in any dispute. Too frequently it is the young man straight from university, using the textbook of psychology and 'understanding the working man', who really causes the trouble. This is how bitter disputes spread.

The ideal Personnel Manager is the man who regards himself not only as the Liaison Officer between management and men, but in one sense he is also a spiritual leader of the very Union to which he appears to stand in opposition. For the business of leadership, and a Personnel Manager is indeed a leader, is to put oneself in the other man's shoes. You watch out for the real grievances, that is those that are rarely mentioned because they apparently have no case, and seek to remedy them before anyone asks about them. That's a Personnel Manager doing his job. He will ask himself why he should not offer increased wages where they are justified, even before they are asked for. He is in as good a position as his own employees, or their union representatives, to know whether there is an economic or social justification for an increase. On examination of the major firms throughout Britain that rarely have a strike record, you will see that the Personnel Manager has called in his shop stewards months before the TUC or the major unions have placed any national claim, and he will have come to terms with his local union, if that is possible, on a local agreement. Of course, this can no longer happen at the time of writing, but history proves that the factory whose Personnel management have been one jump ahead of the economic demand have removed from enemies, either of the country or industry, their weapon of strikes which destroy trust and engender bitterness, not only against management but against authority as a whole. Such leadership exists even now, based on understanding, knowledge and love of men and women. The more the Church recognises the significance of that word 'love' in an industrial situation, the more we shall come closer to that kind of mutual trust which so deeply characterises the foundation and fundamental principles of all our great national institutions. The Personnel Manager who breaks his word with his opposite number, the Factory Convenor, sometimes wins a very temporary victory. What he does is create an enemy in the heart as well as in the mind. A Convenor who has reported to his Committee and then has to go back on his word is a Convenor who has lost dignity. Dignity is as important to him as it is to the Personnel Manager, and the Personnel Manager who forgets this will regret it, nothing is more certain.

Too frequently the Personnel Director toadies to a troublesome Convenor. A man who is a Communist is not necessarily troublesome, and the Personnel Manager will meet someone who is often charming and appears to agree with most of what he says. At the back of his mind is the thought, 'Industry has nothing to do with politics. This man is very useful to me.' But what he forgets is that a man's politics are very often his religion, his faith. Whether he be a Christian or a Communist or an International Socialist or a Fascist, all too frequently all that he does and says has the end product in view, and that is bound up with his ideology. British employers of the 1940s and '50s and part of the '60s have largely themselves to blame for the mess that industry is in at the present time, in the way that they toadied to the trouble-causer. Look back at the 'great names' and the reader can see for himself the men who were respected by employers. Was it respect, or was it toadying to someone who might not cause trouble if they were befriended? Management must never forget that the national interests of industry are more important than profits, and to concede to the whims of a bullying Communist shop steward in order to have industrial peace more often than not is a temporary solution. There are two major dangers management should avoid. One is to concede to an unjust demand in order to avert a politically motivated strike, and the other danger is to refuse a genuine just claim because the trade union leader is a good man who does not wish to see strike action take place.

So much for Personnel Management. What are the Christian implications? Clearly, they are dependant upon a man and his fundamental belief, his faith. Each one of us must act on every occasion.

APPENDIX B

Portrait of a Movement

Tom Chapman describes the picture

The axiom of this Movement is to turn the hearts and minds of men to God that they may walk in His ways. We will not allow these words to be a platitude. We can see a vision of what the words mean. This picture, which deliberately has no title, explains that vision as I described it to the artist, Charles Hardaker.

The tarmacadam road at the bottom of the picture represents the road of life. There is no beginning to the road and no ending. It is symbolic of the path of life. We know not whence we came, nor do we know precisely where we will go at the end or what is in store. Too many walk blindly along that road. The gate has no latch and stands slightly open. We see it as the gateway of choice, and the path leads the walker to the Truth, should he so wish. He alone decides. The path of Truth is not an easy one: notice the question-mark? It is easy to stray towards the edge of the cliff. On one side of the path one can see the decay and the forces of evil at work. There is the deadly nightshade, the rotting tree. At the top of the bend, as in life, there is the tempting opportunity to take the flat and easier road, but it leads to the cliff. If we carry on it is still an uphill climb, but such is the way of Truth. We reach the house. A church? A chapel? A synagogue? We see it as the House of God. The path ahead is obscured by the green leaves of the tree of life. What is beyond is not clearly defined. Through a gap in the trees we see a figure: could it be our Lord Jesus Christ? (I believe it is.) Certainly it is a Messiah.

This is a picture of life; each of us has freedom of choice. The commitment of the Movement to God is symbolised throughout the picture. Some of us must be specially trained to protect the lamb shown caught in the thicket, to lift it to the security of the path or even further over to the green pastures of Truth. Others within the Movement are trained to meet and fight the wolf and keep it from the path, that the seeker after Truth may be protected. Some persuade the sheep standing near the gate not to return to the tarmacadam road. This is the major purpose of oration groups. From such oration comes the uniqueness which each one of us has within his heart, latent but nevertheless available, if we so choose, to the greater work of God.

All of us must be prepared to serve the Messiah in His work to bring the sheep to His fold. This symbolic picture links with the reality of economic and social problems when we understand it as a vision of the road to Truth and the ways of God, for God is concerned with the whole of His creation. Our business is God's business. God's business works through the power of love. That power is realistic, not sentimental or sanctimonious. It must be implemented through the agencies of education, participation, government and worship.

APPENDIX C

The Bridge Builders*

Notes on a talk by James Armstrong, OBE, FREng
Chairman of the Trustees of the ECIM, January 1972

A man stands on the site of a bridge in India. The monsoon has broken. Visibility is down to 20 yards. He is up to his ankles in mud and he knows that below his feet there is 150 feet of sinking sand. Once a year the Indus floods and washes out the bed of the river by which he is standing. The task of building a bridge across the Indus seems insurmountable. The resources of the neighbourhood are very few and poor, the sand is bad, the rock is bad, the people are unskilled in the art of bridge building. They are confused about the purpose of the bridge. They are confused about their own role. They are anxious to ensure their own safety and the safety of their families. They want to get as much out of this bridge for themselves as they can.

On this place, and in this environment, it is difficult for men to build bridges, and this bridge in fact never got built. It is like many bridges that never get built, but this does not stop men wanting to build bridges. It does not mean that there is no need for bridges. It does not mean that we should not continue to try to build bridges.

A bridge builder is a servant. He does not himself propose that certain bridges are needed or certain bridges should be built. He is told by the society in which he lives that a bridge is needed, and that it is his job to build it. So the first thing a man has to know before he would build bridges is that it is not his bridge that is being built, it is not his interests that are being served, it is the needs of the society in which he finds himself. This is important if he is to advise them correctly, if he is to build safely. He must himself, before building, understand the need of the society very well indeed. He must know what it is that is wanted, who is to cross the bridge, what is the scale of the task.

The purpose of a bridge is not just to link two pieces of land across a difficult river or a wide ravine, it is to link people. It is to link people to people so that collectively they may achieve more than they could achieve individually.

---

*This lecture was the inspiration for the name Bridgebuilders, adopted by the ECIM.

In coming to terms with the need for the bridge, he has to understand many things and to survey many things. He next turns his attention to the whole situation of the bridge itself. The situation includes first of all a survey of the site. This means that he must get to know all there is to be known about the neighbourhood and about the people on either bank. He must know how wide and how deep is the river. He must know how fast and how slowly it can flow. He must know what its habits are as far as floods are concerned, whether it swings to this bank or that bank or flows steadily down the middle. He must cross it many times in order to fully understand its nature and how best it can be overcome. He must also know the nature of the ground on either side: how firm are the banks, how deep is the rock, on what should the bridge stand. He must know also what materials are available with which he can build. Is there good rock from which he can make concrete? Can he obtain steel? Should he use timber? Is there stone for an arch? Is there sand? Is there gravel? What is the quality of the water?

He must know what are the skills of the men. Are they skilled in timber or in masonry? Are there men available who know steel, who know how to make it, how to handle it, how to joint it?

These are the nature of the surveys that the bridge builder must carry out. He must do this very objectively – there is no room for wishful thinking because men's lives are at stake. He must see things clearly. He must stand back from the situation himself. Because his last bridge was concrete, and the one before that and the one before that, he must not therefore assume that this bridge must also be concrete. Every situation is different and every man must judge for himself the nature of the problem, and the best means of solving it.

He must stand clear and look.

He must also test the climate of the neighbourhood. Is it wet or dry, are there many gales? Perhaps it is subject to hurricanes or earthquakes. Perhaps the weather is so bitter in the winter that no building can take place. All these factors will be taken into account and in all these factors, when we consider the problems of joining man to man in any social situation, we see the parallels.

We must know our strengths and our weaknesses. We must know the strength of the principles upon which we stand. We must enumerate these clearly, repeat them to ourselves constantly, learn them so that they become deep in our hearts – a firm foundation from which we can move and make our approaches to the other bank, the other man. We must recognise the strength of his principles and ask him to lend us his strength in making this bridge.

So now we have seen the situation. This has taken us many months perhaps, but we cannot rush this situation. We must know fully what we do; but we do and we can start to consider the form of this bridge. We can select the material of which it is to be made. We can look for instance at the quality of steel. The steel that is used most often in building bridges is known as mild steel. It is known as mild steel because it has a quality of yielding and allowing the stress to flow from one part to another. It is not hard and brittle, it is mild. It is well tempered and well understood. It is not a new steel. It has been tried and tested in the works of man for many years. The quality of this steel is even and regular and if we are to build bridges man to man, then we also must be mild, even, well regulated. There is no room for hard and brittle men in this work that we do.

Having yielded to suit the local pressures that come upon us, we must not then give way. This steel is strong; it knows its strength; it stands on that strength; it does not budge.

So also must we men that would build bridges know our own strength, be regular, be consistent and be, in the end, unbending although we might yield a little, to make things easier, to make life smoother, to make it less harsh.

When we arrange the material that we have chosen to suit the nature of the bridge, we must know the laws of bridge building. We must know the natural laws of the materials we use and we must know, of course, of the law of gravity. It is natural for all things to be pulled down to the earth but it is natural for man to stand up straight, to recognise this pull as natural, but not to allow it to prevent his growth. Knowing these laws we can arrange the material so that our solution of the design of the bridge is effective, makes full use of all the material but does not overstress it. We must ensure that we do not ask of the materials we are using more than they can give, but we must also ensure that we ask of them all that they can give so that we make best use of all that is available.

We have now designed our bridge and we move on to its construction. So far the team of men working on this project may have been quite small – a few men skilled in the various arts and sciences of survey, of appraising the situation, a few men of goodwill and earnest intent who can carry through this project, but now we need the help of all men, for the construction of a major bridge requires many men. It requires working men, men that know how to work, that know the importance of the job they are doing and who get on with this job.

They must be able to co-operate with each other fully; they much appreciate the value of teamwork and in bridge building, as in any other major engineering work, we see this co-operation very clearly. Men know that their lives and the lives of their fellows depend upon the quality of their work and so they will work well and willingly together, so long as they know the full nature of the task they have in hand.

When we are confused or doubtful or when the nature of the job has not been fully explained then they find it difficult. Then they wonder at the peculiar nature of some of their fellows, and they themselves behave less perfectly because their knowledge is less complete and so co-operation depends upon a willing understanding of the whole situation in which men find themselves. When this understanding is present there are no problems of discipline because men are not working for themselves but for the job as a whole. If we are to build bridges we must realise that we are working for the job as a whole, not to create a monument for ourselves. We do not want to build a bridge which is capable of carrying only a statue to ourselves and not of joining men from bank to bank. Perhaps, above all, men that build bridges need strength. This strength, of course, is an inner strength, a strength of purpose, a strength of principle. It breeds men who are steadfast, who remain true to the task and who are above all at all times aware of their manhood.

We are approaching the need and the situation of linking nations one with the other within this great continent of Europe. At one level as we look around we see that there are many differences between people, there are differences of habits, of customs, of language. There are differences in histories: one nation has won a war which means that another has lost it. These produce different attitudes in the hearts of men. We note that there are 20 million in this nation, 60 million in that and 50 million in the other and we realise that many men make great nations, but above all we should realise that any man is greater than any nation and in doing this we will not feel that our bank of the river is better than the other man's bank because we know that the man who crosses the bridge is greater than both banks, and this is part of the bridge builder's ability to stand back.

Arising out of this simple analogy of bridge building, come four or five factors and these we can apply to any situation in which we find ourselves:

We must first stand clear.
We must then know the need.
We must then know the place.
We can then know the form.
Then we can build.

APPENDIX D

Our Common Future
Conference address by Roger Pincham, CBE
27th December 1989

In asking me to contribute to Our Common Future, Tom suggested that I focus my sights firmly upon the world to be inherited by my grandchildren. As such children belong still to the realm of conjecture, I am thinking immediately of two small great-nephews with whom we spent a wonderful Christmas Day. The elder, Oliver, aged just three, is already sensitive to the starving children in Ethiopia, and when comforted not to worry, insists, 'But I *am* worried, Mummy.'

The same sentiment was expressed by a young freedom fighter in Romania, who made the sign of the Cross upon learning of the execution of the Ceausescus and explained, 'We are still young enough to feel compassion.'

When my great-nephews and my conjectured grandchildren come to history lessons at school, the year 1989 will be remembered as one of the turning points in human history. The cause of the sudden revulsion against tyranny will no doubt be the subject of learned theses for many years to come. The influence of radio and television, the unity and prosperity of the West, the economic crisis in Russia and the inner workings of President Gorbachev's mind – all these will be cited as contributory factors. But, in essence, we have been witnessing the triumph of the human spirit nourished, as throughout the centuries, by faith in God. Throughout Eastern Europe it has been the churches, whether Catholic, Protestant or Orthodox, which have kept hope alive with a truer and more noble vision of human life created in the image of God. This vision has been held in the teeth of a form of government whose drabness had been a cover for gross corruption and tyranny.

Political change can be effected by a sudden surge of popular revolution or the fall of the guillotine. But the process of rebuilding shattered communities and restoring the supplies of goods and services which we take for granted, will be the work of a generation. The same generosity of spirit which inspired unarmed young people to shed their blood in Timisoara and Bucharest will be required in the long process of binding up wounds and, above all, in forgiving the terrible past deeds of oppressors whose future can only lie in the same communities. Prior to the revolution in Romania, I could only marvel at the restraint and co-operation which had been shown elsewhere in the Eastern Bloc, despite the great emotional charge of recent events. The knowledge that destruction leads only to destruction is essential to the survival of the human race.

Besides these great changes, the differences within our own political system seem puny and almost parochial. None of our political parties seems by itself to command the qualities to meet the challenges of the future. For example, recent events in Eastern Europe have demonstrated both the abiding strength and virtue of nationhood as a force for good in human affairs as well as the utter interdependence of nations upon each other in meeting the deep needs of humanity. I can therefore only sympathise with those who are anxious that the vigorous sovereignty of the United Kingdom should not be exchanged for provincial status within a great bureaucratic European federation. Even more, I abhor the notion of a selfish, loutish, small-minded Britain concerned mainly with her own narrow interests.

Of course Britain must not shirk her role in building a liberal, democratic and secure Europe. But the world will be poorer if we do this at the expense of turning our backs on the community of English-speaking nations with whom we share so much common heritage.

Again, as much as we may rejoice at the demise of Marxism, we should not forget, nor should we let others forget, that its seedbed was the poverty, injustice, ignorance and tyranny of earlier times. Few thinking people can now believe that the future prosperity of mankind or the future health of the planet will be secured simply by a general acceptance of unbridled market forces or the right to limitless private indulgence.

If the common future of our grandchildren and great grandchildren – and their contemporaries throughout the world – is to be based upon freedom from fear of want or war, and by the positive freedoms of speech, thought, worship and expression, an immense amount of work remains to be done by all of us in our own generation. It is no time to sit back and gloat over the fall of dictators.

The task is to renew the world's vision of a peaceful social order with liberty, compassion and devotion to justice as its bedrocks. These virtues will ensure material plenty. It is time to rediscover the immortal values which are the natural guides of Man's mortal life. Then *our common future* will deserve to see the fulfilment of the great upsurge of hope which has been fired by human courage in these last momentous months of 1989.

APPENDIX E

Divinity Shines in Every Heart

Closing speech delivered by Tom Chapman, Wadderton Conference, Blackwell, 30th March, 1969

Divinity shines in every heart. It is not only within. It is without. It is everywhere. But in the heart it shines in its purity, without blemish or fault.

There is the fullness of Knowledge in its perfection. Only through this may a man know the Truth about anything.

Every man believes that he can penetrate to the truth of something or other if he really wants to and is prepared to make the effort. This belief arises from this pure light.

There also is happiness, eternal and absolute. This is the source of all happiness. People ascribe their happiness to all sorts of things but they are mistaken. Happiness does not depend on anything. A happy man is happy everywhere and in every situation. The most miserable man is happy some time in spite of himself. This is because of that supreme light shining in the heart. It is the source of all happiness everywhere.

Our Lord said, 'The Kingdom of God is within you.' The wise of every land have proclaimed it. We are in a very real sense God's creatures.

This is the light which leads the good man through the perplexities of life and keeps him firm and strong through all adversity. From it comes life and strength abounding, equal to any task. The wise declare that this is the Supreme Knowledge. Who knows it will not taste death.

Only the dark shadow of ignorance hanging over the world obscures this Knowledge from the mind and heart so that men do not know it. This ignorance is the cause of all suffering and misery. It perverts the Divine Power in the hearts of men into the forces of evil and destruction. It is this same power only perverted.

However evil a man's ways have become, he may yet turn to good ways if he still breathes. This possibility arises from that pure light which is not extinguished.

The ignorant man, bent on wicked ways, has one fatal weakness, however powerful he appears to be. His weakness is his ignorance. In the end this defeats him. The strength of the good man is Knowledge and Love.

Love flows from this same Divinity which is everywhere and it flows from the heart because that Divinity is reflected there in its purity. It is the intangible force which binds creation together. Its action is to unite. Its nature is to seek nothing for itself. It is prepared to give everything. It shows itself in an all-pervading care. This care reaches down to the tiniest details. Every man has felt this strange care protecting his steps in life. It is the joy in fine craftsmanship, in children and the home. Enmity, anxiety, conceit and envy dissolve and disappear in it. Saint John said 'God is Love.'

In their ignorance people seek knowledge, everlasting happiness, fullness of life and love everywhere, not realising it is within. This is what causes all the activity in the world. They seek it in learning, riches, dominion over others, in pursuits of all kinds, in friends, lovers, crowds, crime and in the most unlikely places. What is more, they seek a special knowledge, a special happiness, a special life, a special love, all for themselves, regardless of what anyone else is going to get. This blind selfishness is how all the trouble gets into the world. But the man who has but caught a glimpse of the true Knowledge, Bliss or Love, or who sees the true richness of life, wants everyone to share it.

Moreover he seeks out others of a like mind as his chosen companions. It is a law that like is attracted to like and it is good that good men should gather together. Good company is all-important. It strengthens and refreshes as nothing else can, for it puts every good man in memory of what he really knows. It renews his confidence, strengthens his resolution and enables him to do what is needful.

Our Lord said, 'Woman, why callest thou me good? There is none good save God.' The goodness in man is the reflection of the Divine Light shining in the heart. Like true Knowledge, Happiness and Love, it is not his, but is of God, as is his life also. And his life is to do the good he knows.

APPENDIX F

Our Common Future

Peter G. Green, BSc (Est Man), FRICS
ECIM Trustee, c.1990

As we see the rending of that Iron Curtain that descended across Europe in the years after the Second World War, there is naturally and rightly great joy and a new sense of hope for the world.

But we need to temper that joy and hope with realism to avoid disillusionment in the years ahead.

From one point of view there should be sadness that communism has failed, for it was the great experiment intended by its founders to replace the injustice of earlier regimes with a brave new world based on liberty, equality and fraternity – all ideals of undoubted worth and goodness. Had feudalism, and later capitalism, not been seen to fail to offer these ideals there would have been no need to seek to convert the world to the socialist doctrine – for communism is, in essence, socialism taken to its logical conclusions.

If we are really objective, we should question why a doctrine based on communal values should fail even more spectacularly than one based on individual values; why the common good should not be a superior goal to the individual good. But it is not in either approach that the fault lies, it is in man himself. If men were filled with goodness and a love of justice, if they observed their duties to their fellow men, then the pursuit of happiness, whether on an individual or communal basis, could not be at the expense of others and would lead naturally to the happiness of all. Equally, if men succumb to greed and selfishness, then those who have power in a communalist society will seek their own advantage just as avidly as those who manipulate a free-market society to their own ends. There has been no less privilege east of the Iron Curtain than to the west – just less general prosperity to carve up to one's advantage and thus even greater hardship for the deprived.

This may all sound cynical. But if we, as Bridgebuilders, would seek to be good citizens, it is very important that we are not caught up so much by the political jousting around us that we miss the real issue – the point where something useful can be done.

Man, made in the image of God, must surely be innately good, but blinded by his own ignorance. That is why he has always relied on revealed knowledge for his guidance, why the voice of the prophets has been so powerful an influence over the ages. That is why the ancient scriptures and the words of the great Teachers have survived the ages; why the words of Jesus during his so-short lifetime have been cherished by the western world for nearly 2000 years as the guide to living. Indeed, it is these very words that are frequently used to defend doctrines of the left and right alike.

Surely the heart of the Christian message is to be found in the commandments of Jesus: 'Love the Lord thy God ... and love thy neighbour as thyself.' We may not be able to have much direct influence on the future political scene of the world, but we can follow or ignore this commandment. Indeed it is worth noting that it is only individual men and women who can love God and love their neighbour – neither democratic governments nor dictatorships can do that, although their laws and edicts can reflect or deny the spirit of the commandments. Jesus put his finger on the real key to human happiness in giving these commandments. That key is in the hands of ordinary men and women like us – millions of them. For everyone seeks happiness – often in the most unlikely ways – and people are attracted by those who radiate happiness. Only those whose hearts are hardened by evil turn from it.

So, from this point of view, our common future is directly in our own hands. If we follow Jesus' commandments there is no room for the short-term interest of the individual at the expense of those around him. Just as the extra drink leads to a hangover or the extra mince pie to a stomach-ache, so seeking my own advantage regardless of others leads to hardheartedness and misery.

'Love the Lord thy God with all they heart, and with all thy soul, and with all thy mind.' What a commandment! How to put this into practice has been discussed by theologians over the ages. But two simple points seem worth noting here. Even a smattering of understanding of this commandment and there will be no doubt that all the gifts of the earth are from God and that all authority is from God. Those two facts, if remembered, change our approach to life. Whose house, whose car, whose money? And with whose authority do we give orders, and whose orders do we receive?

The second commandment is complementary to the first and probably the key to where to find God, for we will surely not find Him by staring into the heavens or searching our imaginations. 'Love thy neighbour as thyself.' Not just 'love thy neighbour', but '... as thyself'. To do that we have to put ourselves in our neighbour's shoes. We cannot do that from a state of introspection or from a desire to be seen to do good. To love our neighbour, we have consideration for our neighbour. First, how do we refrain from impinging on his freedom to enjoy the world, then, if he needs our positive help, how do we give it?

Who is our neighbour? – not only the man or woman next door, but also the man or woman in front of us. We find our neighbour in the bus, at work, in the shops, at our Church, wherever we go. There is no need to seek – just deal with whatever is presented, however unlikely. Consideration will ensure that we are not a nuisance to our neighbour, do not offend, do not take unfair advantage. In other words, do not do to our neighbour the things we would not want done to us – and further, do not do the things we would not want done to us *if we were in their place*. We may not mind noise or an untidy garden or a dubious remark, but our neighbour may.

Then let all our business dealings be fair – whether as shopper or trader, employee or employer, client or professional; we have a duty to the other to play fair – even if we think nobody else does. For some of us, this means not passing on the dud coin we found in our change, for others it means fair play in agreeing a wage claim for a thousand men. The principle does not change.

Our neighbours, wherever we meet them, may be in real need – need of comfort, need of a meal, need of encouragement, need of just a word of greeting; and, like all of us, they each need respect and to be allowed the dignity due to a human being. Just as love of a child may call for the sharp slap from time to time, so love of our neighbour may call for a few sharp words and a reminder of some home truths, but given without rancour. Again, consideration of the person and not of my own convenience is the key throughout. Sometimes it is best to wait and watch, sometimes to act now; somehow if we are quiet within we know what has to be done. We should follow that knowledge and not listen to our personal prejudices. Whether we like our neighbour or not has to be set aside as irrelevant. Jesus' commandment accepts no exceptions.

Back to the first commandment. The love of God leads us into actions which are not for my own gain, not because they make me feel good but just because they are there to be done. Action which meets a need but carries no reward for me is to the benefit of all and strengthens the love of God.

A thousand Bridgebuilders following those commandments as best they can – what an effect that would have. We have already seen at our conferences how this magic works when we are together and many already practice this in their daily lives. But we could all take it so much further. As we meet the needs that are presented to us, so we shall find that more is asked of us. As we join some useful activity, or are asked to sit on a Trades Union Committee or an Employers' Committee, to join the local Parent-Teacher Association or the Board of Governors, to stand for the Local Council or become secretary of the Mothers Union branch – so the opportunity enlarges. We do not necessarily want to seek power or influence, but if it is offered or thrust upon us we should not refuse it and should put it to good use.

Our common future is, by definition, largely the future of our neighbours – that determines our own future. Care for our common future will lead us to the good, whilst care for our individual tomorrows can only lead to continuing human misery. The present is a time of exceptional opportunity – for good or ill. Let us not miss it, but work together for the greater good.

APPENDIX G

Scargill
21st January 1973
Extract from a speech by Dr Sergei Tarassenko

Through the ages, man has been investigating the universe on a cosmic scale. In very early days, at the beginning of man's history, the evolution process was predominant. Nowadays, man seeks a conscious and readily accepted evolution, a controlled process towards positive progress, towards our good. Therefore, he rationalises his effort to comprehend the universe; that is to say, he tries to perceive the universe with the help of the most sophisticated scientific instruments. Then he stores and processes the information collected. And he *thinks* – in other words he reflects the processed information against the mirror of his mind; and he builds a model – that is he makes up a coherent and consistent picture the purpose of which is to explain in a logical way the phenomena as observed. Such a picture, such a model is endlessly improved so that, in the end, he has a sophisticated tool to manipulate, and finally he is in a position to observe the universe in better conditions and more accurately.

The question is, however, what does he really know? What kind of truth does he in fact embrace? For he holds only a set of highly refined models, a collection of sophisticated pictures, and that is *all!* Indeed, those tools are very useful. For example, the model which describes the complicated field of attractions between objects and planets, called the theory of gravitation, enables him to send rockets and spacecraft beyond the earth's atmosphere and to recover them at a point accurately predicted in space and time. The model describing the structure of matter helps him to extract the best from the energy resources trapped in matter. The model of the electromagnetic field is of paramount importance in developing telecommunications. And what development over the past 50 years! Yesterday a squeaking transreceiver, with a range of only several miles, at the disposal of a handful of privileged people – and now! Millions of people all around the world watching on their TV sets a programme transmitted by satellite of a man walking on the surface of the moon! ...

But a model remains a picture and embraces nothing. We are still without an answer as to the purpose of life. Is our destiny only to be born, to work, to enjoy life and to die – in other words to disappear without any connection with anything everlasting? Why are we so blind and miserable in that respect?

I would rather think that the answer to such a question lies in our own innermost depths ...

APPENDIX H

Westminster Conference
1975
Extracts from speeches

Man and his achievements have to be measured against the scale of eternity, the dimension of everlasting life, and everything has to be measured against that scale.

Dr Sergei Tarassenko

If we do not get inspiration from God – God who is in whatever we say, we hear, we do – we cannot live. As St Paul said, 'In God we have Life, Movement and Being'. The image is that of the Cross; we have the vertical line – in the words of St Paul, 'Life, Movement and Being.' If we do not understand the vertical line we are nowhere. For whoever believes in God, nothing human is strange.

Our faith would be speculative if we were not interested in everyday problems of people. That is why our objective has to be the intersection of the two lines of the Cross. It is the nucleus – the crossroads where we can find the solution to the problems of Christianity today.

We remember that God is Life in the vertical line, but that we have to keep all of mankind and all human problems in our hearts: remember this.

Père Marie-Joseph Pudor

It has been necessary for trades unions over the last hundred years or so to develop a very strong sense of corporate loyalty, but this has developed to such an extent that these horizontal loyalties in trades unions, and indeed in professional associations, jell up together on their own level and nothing will affect the loyalty of each member to his group. Now this has potentialities for great good, but it also has potentialities for evil, because in addition to horizontal loyalties we need vertical loyalties. We need loyalties that go up and down as well as across; ultimately to God Himself as our maker. Loyalty to our nation symbolised by loyalty to the crown, loyalty to our firm, loyalty to our university, loyalty to our school, and so on. All these other loyalties are vertical loyalties. There is something wrong with society if all the loyalties are vertical or all the

113

loyalties are horizontal. The sign of our religion is a Cross – and a cross speaks of horizontal loyalties and also of vertical loyalties. We look up to God and to our leaders, while we also embrace all those who share our particular task or responsibility in the world.

> The Rt Revd Ronald Williams, DD,
> The Bishop of Leicester

Leadership must start at the top. It must come from the people who are entrusted with power and responsibility. Though leadership involves all sections of society, you cannot expect the layman to give a lead if the people who have responsibility and power do not have the guts to give it also.

> Jack Peel, CBE

APPENDIX I

Common Cause

Hugh Lunghi

Common Cause was incorporated as a limited company in December 1952 and shortly thereafter a brief statement in *The Times* announced its existence. Its head office was in London where it remained in modest premises until the mid-seventies when it moved to an even more modest office in Fleet, Hampshire.

There was nothing clandestine about the leaflet publicly distributed in 1953 urgently calling for support. It correctly claimed the new body to be the only non-party organisation with extensive trades union support fighting communism; its Council included 'leading members of the three major parties and non-party individuals of national and international repute'. Its Industrial Committee consisted of 'trade unionists only'.

It aimed to maintain in Britain 'the democratic freedoms on which our civilisation is based' and, somewhat ambitiously, 'to develop them elsewhere and restore them where they have been destroyed'. It recognised that the destruction of fascism had not removed the threat to freedom, 'now in peril from the spread of communism through the combination of armed attack and internal undermining of states by national Communist Parties under Soviet control'.

From *The Common Cause Story*
Common Cause Ltd, London, 1995, p.13

Appendix J

Love and Truth

Towards the Millennium
ECIM Grange-over-Sands Conference, 1996

This very successful conference addressed the general theme of human requirements in the next millennium. Six crucial institutions of community life were considered, the quality of each of which has a profound effect upon the quality of life in any society. Following the penetrating reports from each of the study groups the following brief summaries were formulated:

CHURCH

It is the duty of the churches to deliver, and not to debate, the Love and Truth in society.

FAMILY

Families should respect their covenant with God to be Loving and Truthful in all their relationships with one another.

INDUSTRY

Industry should praise all honest and well intentioned endeavour, thus encouraging working relationships based upon Love and Truth, and not only upon profit.

LAW

The primary responsibility of local institutions is to maintain Love and Truth in society, not merely to regulate human weaknesses.

EDUCATION

The primary aim of education at all stages is to assist in the discovery of the Love and Truth embodied in all human beings, to develop an integrated, not a divided society.

YOUTH

The energy and generosity of Youth should be deployed to support their vision of a society based on Love and Truth, not conflict and exploitation.

Taken from the April 1996 *ECIM Newsletter*

APPENDIX K

Extracts from ECIM Newsletters
Tom Chapman
1998-2001

July 1998

Dear Friends,

Once again I feel I must declare I make no pretence of being a theologian. This Newsletter will be written according to the advice given to me by the first Bishop who advised me to write what was in my heart, after a long talk with GOD and not before. Make sure the content is His, not mine. Once written, leave it to the Holy Spirit. Every Newsletter written in the last forty years has obeyed that Law ...

January 2000

Beloved Friends,

Most of the first half of my generation were convinced we would never live to see the beginning of this Millennium and here we are. Hence more than ever and doubly so we can heartily wish a Happy, happy, joyous Christmas and a thrilling, exciting New Year to every one of God's worldwide children, in God's wishes. Indeed, it is God's Will that there are no exceptions. For those who think there are, reaching their hearts and minds is one of our objectives.

Let there be no mistake. May I assure my generation, we have not passed our 'sell-by date'. God has a purpose for every one of us, just as there is a purpose for every child being born at this minute. The Kingdom of Heaven can be likened to a huge jigsaw puzzle and every one of us is a piece of it ...

September 2001

On the door of our lovely Church, where I love to worship whenever possible, there has been for some months now a hand printed message which reads as follows: 'Woe unto us if we preach religion instead of the Gospel'. These words fill my mind each time I prepare a Newsletter.

October 2001

Indeed, the world is a different place since Tuesday, 11th September 2001. I want us to look at what we can do in our own hearts, in our community and in our nations to eliminate anything that could cause hatred. This is a time to embrace and give, wholeheartedly, to share all we have. We are trading, travelling and communicating in the global village. A village is a community where everybody is our neighbour. This is the neighbour our Lord Jesus Christ commands us to love. No provision is made for exclusion of the neighbour who looks different, has different customs or worships the Lord our Father in a different way, under a different name. Such differences are superficial and melt away in our common humanity, in the image of God.

November 2001

It begins with a smile. A smile is like a ray of sunshine on a rainy day. A smile is what you give and every person you meet and every pet and even insects, plants and stones are happy with a smile. And it's contagious. A smile is a reflection of the Divine Light shining in every heart.

Then, my opinion of you is more important that your opinion of me. In other words, it does not matter so much what I feel about what someone seems to think or say about me; what is important is that I do not criticise others but praise their qualities and good deeds. If I do not worry about 'my feelings' I am free to love whoever I meet, and ready to respond to any need.

The rest you leave in the hands of God.

Notes

INTRODUCTION
1. Estimates of total Soviet military and civilian deaths in the period 1941-5 stand at more than 25 million. See Richard Overy, *Russia's War*, Penguin, London, 1999.
2. *Dictionary of National Biography 1931-40*, Oxford University Press, London, 1949, p.823.
3. A.J.P. Taylor, *English History 1914-1945*, Clarendon Press, Oxford, 1965, pp.244-5.
4. *Ibid*, p.195.
5. Hugh Lunghi, *The Common Cause Story*, Common Cause Ltd, 28 Ely Place, London EC1, 1995, p.10 (ISBN 0906587050).
6. *Ibid*, p.5.

CHAPER 2
1. Thomas à Kempis, *The Imitation of Christ*, Penguin Books, London, 1968, p.55.
2. George Orwell, *The Road to Wigan Pier*, Penguin Books, London, 1962, p.45.
3. The Tom Chapman papers.*
4. A.J.P. Taylor, *English History 1914-1945*, Clarendon Press, Oxford, 1965, pp.244-5.
5. *Ibid*, p.248.

CHAPER 3
1. *Encyclopaedia Britannica*.

CHAPTER 6
1. Sidney Silverman, LLB, MP (Labour Party MP for Nelson and Colne).
2. Hugh Lunghi, *The Common Cause Story*, Common Cause, London, 1995, p.22.

---

*All quotations of Tom's words are from the Tom Chapman papers.

CHAPTER 7

1. Anthony Lejeune, 'Communism in British Trade Unions: The Facts', *Reader's Digest*, September 1967, p.41.
2. Hugh Lunghi, *The Common Cause Story*, Common Cause, London, 1995, p.23. Extract from the first bi-monthly publication under the title *IRIS News*, September 1956, then the industrial wing of Common Cause (IRIS being Industrial Research and Information Services Ltd).
3. Anthony Lejeune, *ibid*, p.46.
4. Hugh Lunghi, *ibid*, p.13. He also writes (p.13): 'After the Soviet Union's collapse in 1991 Russian publications and documents released there confirmed that communist parties and their supporters in Western countries had been given money clandestinely with orders to disrupt and destroy the economy of their own countries. For anyone prepared to look and listen the Soviet media had been putting over the message of disruption clearly enough ever since the start of the 'Fifties.'
5. No known relationship to the Miss Glading who introduced Tom to Leon MacLaren.
6. General Secretary of the Amalgamated Union of Engineering Workers. He was killed in an air crash in 1974.

CHAPTER 8

1. William Temple, *Christianity and Social Order*, Shepheard-Walwyn (Publishers) Ltd, London, 1976, p.77. (First published by Penguin Books, 1942.)

CHAPTER 9

1. Frank Chapple, *Sparks Fly!* Michael Joseph, London, 1984, p.195.
2. President of the Amalgamated Union of Engineering Workers; created Baron by James Callaghan.
3. Hugh Lunghi, *The Common Cause Story*, Common Cause, London, 1995, p.36.
4. The School of Economic Science.
5. *The Times*, 15th May 2002, Business section, p.27, article entitled 'Union Establishment Faces Poll Showdown', by Christine Buckley, on current union politics: '... Many recent union elections, which have delivered the "awkward squad" of new generation union leaders ... have been won on an appetite for change ...' See also *The Times*, Wednesday, 4th September 2002, Business section, p.23, and leader, 2nd December 2002.

CHAPTER 10

1. *The Oxford Dictionary of Quotations*, Second Edition, Oxford University Press, London, p.167 (26).
2. Tom Grundy, *The Global Miracle of Float Glass*, Tom Grundy, St Helens, 1990 (ISBN 0951697900).
3. John Ritson, *The Pilkington Dispute*, Macdonald & Evans Ltd, London, 1973, p.15 (Appendix 11).
4. Dr Lawrence Peter, *Quotations for Our Time* (British Edition), Souvenir Press, London, 1978, p.53.
5. Alfred J. Mapp, Jr, *Thomas Jefferson, Passionate Pilgrim*, Madison Books, Lanham, Maryland, 1991, p.366.

CHAPTER 11

1. William Temple, *Christianity and Social Order*, Shepheard-Walwyn, London, 1976, p.75.
2. *Hansard*, 11th February 1971, col.814.
3. The Revd John Oldham, Priest in Charge, St Bartholomews, Derby, 1964-72.
4. Charles Hunt, Works Convenor, Rolls-Royce, Derby. See *Derby Evening Telegraph*, 17th February 1971 (front page photograph).
5. *Hansard*, 11th February 1971, col.883.
6. *The Times*, 12th November 1970, p.25 (final paragraph of leader).
7. This was a bitter dispute. See *The Times*, 5th December 1968. Arthur Hearsey, Tom's friend and one of the twelve young men, was involved.
8. *The Times*, 6th February 1976.
9. International Socialists.
10. The only substantial diary entry. Tom was not a diarist.

CHAPTER 12

1. In 1977 Douglas Thomas was employed by the London Borough of Bromley as a Management Services Officer responsible for running a number of incentive bonus schemes, mainly for tradesmen in the Council's Housing and Architects' Departments. He was also a rather reluctant NALGO Departmental Representative (or shop steward). No one else would do the job!
2. Extract from a letter posted to the ECIM at the news of Tom's death.

CHAPTER 13

1. Sir David Lancaster Nicolson FIC, FEng (1922-96), Chairman of numerous companies during his long career, including Vickers Shipbuilding & Engineering plc; first Chairman of British Airways, responsible for the merger of BEA and BOAC; European Advisor to the New York Stock Exchange and a member of the CBI Council; Governor of Imperial College, London for eleven years, and also a Fellow; and Member of the European Parliament for five years.
2. Sir Patrick Dean, GCMG, 1963. He was a Director of Taylor Woodrow, 1969-86, and International Adviser for American Express. He practised at the Bar 1934-9, was UK Permanent Representative to the United Nations, 1960-4, and Ambassador in Washington, 1965-9. He was a Member of the Departmental Committee set up to examine the operation of Section 2 of the Official Secrets Act, 1971; Deputy President of the English-Speaking Union, 1984-94; a member of the Governing Body of Rugby School, 1939-84 (and Chairman 1972-84); an Honorary Fellow of Clare College and Gonville and Caius College, Cambridge, 1965; and Honorary Bencher at Lincoln's Inn, 1965.
3. Jack Peel, CBE, 1972. He was General Secretary of the Union of Dyers, Bleachers and Textile Workers, 1966-73; a member of the TUC General Council, 1966-72; Director of Industrial Relations, EEC Social Affairs Directorate, 1973-9; and a member of the Industrial Committee of the Board of Social Responsibility when Tom Chapman was Liaison Officer.
4. Dr Sergei Tarassenko, nuclear physicist. He was born on 7th October 1935 in Versailles, France, of exiled parents, both of whom were political refugees from Eastern bloc countries, and became a naturalised British citizen in 1983. He had a Doctorate in Applied Nuclear Physics and was employed as a nuclear physicist by the French Atomic Energy Authority from 1956; in 1970-83 he was seconded by the French Ministry of Science and Technology to the Dragon and JET projects; in 1984-7 he was a consultant on the ARIANE 5 programme for nuclear power generation in space. From 1967 he was guest speaker for a wide variety of organisations (including political and parliamentary groups, trades unions, Christian churches of all denominations, student Christian Unions and industrial Christian associations) on the theme: 'The message of the Gospel, a searching light for mankind living in a scientific age'.
5. The Christian International Peace Service, CHIPS, places teams at grass-roots level in areas of tension to work creatively for harmony and co-operation between conflicting communities, for example through agricultural projects. Tom would have appreciated this grass-roots approach.
6. George Ward, Personnel and Training Officer for Rockwell Glass. He later became involved in Government Youth Opportunity Schemes.

7. The Corrymeela Community, founded by Dr Ray Davey, Presbyterian Chaplain to Queen's University, in 1965 as a group for reconciliation. It is based on the County Antrim coast near Ballycastle where a sign proclaims: 'Corrymeela starts when you go home'.
8. During the visit Tom maintained that he was shadowed by a Communist from Britain.
9. Christian Schumacher (a strong supporter of Tom) was on the Industrial Committee of the Board of Social Responsibility when Tom was Liaison Officer. He is the author of *God in Work*, Lion Publishing, Oxford, 1998. Written in the form of a memoir, this book is easy to read and records his efforts to establish Christian organisational structures in the workplace.

CHAPTER 14

1. The Revd William Gowland, Founder Principle of Luton Industrial College, 1957-85, President of the Methodist Conference 1978-80 and ECIM Patron, c.1986. He died on 23rd May 1991.
2. See Chapter 10, p.44 (last two lines of page).
3. *The Graphic and Creative Arts Association, Report 2*, February 1983 (front page).
4. Official calligrapher to St Pauls Cathedral.
5. From the report by Don Bruce.

CHAPTER 15

1. Industrial Notes No. 76.
2. Words of the Revd William J.H. Boetcker, who lectured in the United States on Industrial Relations at the turn of the 20th Century, later wrongly attributed to Abraham Lincoln. (See Abraham Lincoln Online speeches and writings – Non-Lincoln 'You Cannot' quotation.)
3. Common Cause Report on 'Politically Correct Class Warfare'.
4. The Revd Basil Watson, OBE, MA, RN. Chaplin RNVR, 1944-6; Royal Navy, 1946-70; Vicar of St Lawrence Jewry, London, 1970-86; Patron of the ECIM from the mid-1980s.

CHAPTER 16

1. Mr and Mrs Schoup ran the School of Philosophy in Brussels.
2. The Focolare Movement was started in Trento, Italy, in 1943 by Chiara Lubich. In the midst of the hatred and violence of the Second World War,

she and her companions set out to rediscover the Gospel and put it into practice in their daily lives. Promoting the 'Spirituality of Unity', the Movement soon spread throughout Italy, then Europe; it is now active throughout the world. It was taken up not only by Christians of different denominations but also by believers of different faiths and by people with no religious conviction, all of whom are committed to solidarity and unity in the world. Approved by the Holy See in 1962 and its successive developments in 1990, it has been officially recognised by the Orthodox Church and the Anglican and Lutheran Churches, by representatives of other religions and by a number of international organisations, all of whom are working together to achieve Jesus' testament 'that all may be one'.

3. Van Ede & Partners, Sophialaan 31, 1075 BL Amsterdam.
4. Marsilio Ficino (1433-99). From him and his Academy the Renaissance drew its most potent intellectual and spiritual inspiration. See Introduction to *The Letters of Marsilio Ficino* Vol 1, Shepheard-Walwyn, London, 1975, p.19.
5. Luc Glorie first trained as a Jesuit priest but, concluding this was not his calling, he became an engineer. Leen, like Verena Watson, is a translator.

CHAPTER 17

1. Robert McNeill, Deputy Head of an old-established boys' school in Lancashire.
2. Andrew Cresswell, RMN, Bsc(Hons), Clinical Service Manager, Child and Adolescent Mental Health Service, Gwent Healthcare NHS Trust; Delyth Cresswell, singing teacher, Junior Music and Access Studies Department, Royal Welsh College of Music and Drama.
3. Spoken at the February 2001 Cumbria Grand Conference.
4. These talks, which began in June 1974 and continued until November 1985, represented a broad spectrum of opinion. The speakers are listed on pp.180-1 of *Airs and Graces*, a delightful and informative book written by the Revd Basil Watson, and published by Ashburnham Publishers, London, 1993 (ISBN 0951090410).
5. Obituary extract, Minutes, Methodist Church Conference, 1991.
6. *Ibid*.
7. Dr James Armstrong, OBE, HonDEng, RAEng, BSc, Past President of the Institution of Structural Engineers. He is an Honorary Fellow of Harris-Manchester College, Oxford and has played an active role in developing educational policies in professional education. He was a Director of a Prince's Trust organisation concerned with inner-city training programmes and is Chairman of the ECIM Trustees.

8. Peter G. Green, BSc(EstMa), FRICS. Past Joint Chief Surveyor of the Prudential Assurance Co; Director of Prudential Portfolio Managers; Past Principal and Chairman of The School of Economic Science.
9. Dr Iain Carincross graduated in Chemistry from Edinburgh University and, after spending a year as a Post-Doctoral Fellow at Iowa State University, joined ICI in their sales and marketing department. He subsequently spent several years as a Management Consultant and thereafter as Managing Director, of a number of companies, finally becoming a Main Board Director of a publicly-quoted plc.
10. Ian D. Mason, BA(Hons), Barrister and Lecturer in Economics.

CHAPTER 18

1. Bill Finley, President of The Speakers Club and Holistic Development at Piekhanov Academy, Moscow (the old Academy of Economics).
2. Alexander Grechaninov, 1864-1956. Tom records that the piece was 'Credo in A', probably from one of the masses.

CHAPTER 19

1. T.E. Lawrence, Seven Pillars of Wisdom, Jonathan Cape, London, 1935, p.356.

CHAPTER 20

1. Louis I. Bredvold & Ralph G. Ross (eds), *The Philosophy of Edmund Burke*, University of Michigan Press, Ann Arbor, 1960, p.16.
2. From the statement of Archbishop William Temple. See William Temple, *Christianity and Social Order*, Shepeard-Walwyn, London, 1976, p.44.
3. Spoken at the 1975 ECIM Conference.

Index

AEF (Amalgamated Union of Engineers and Foundrymen) 36, 38
AEU (Amalgamated Engineering Union) xi, 8, 20, 22, 25, 29
Barrow-in-Furness:
  Tom's boyhood 3
  Apprenticeship 7, 9-11
  Vickers 13, 18, 92
  the Strike 36-8
  Tom in hospital 59
  Tom retires to Stainton 72
Barrow News x, 36, 38
Bevan, Nye xiv
Bevin, Ernest xiv, 6
Board of Social Responsibility (Church of England):
  Tom invited to Ripon Hall 29
  Tom's reports 34, 37, 47
  Tom leaves 35
  Jack Peel 76
Burke, Edmund 44, 84
Calvocoressi, Roy 54
Cassandra (*Daily Mirror* columnist) x, 21, 22
Castle, Barbara 75
Chapple, Frank 36, 60
Chapman, Pat
  marriage to Tom 20
  support in difficult times 23
  Tom's busy life 34
  Cumbria Grand years 72-3
Chapman, Tom
  birth 3
  childhood conditions 4-5
  King James Bible 6
  twelve young men 7-8
  guidance from the Revd Stannard 9-11
  views on respect 12-14
  friendship with Bob Hornwell 15

Chapman, Tom—*contd*
  Bible study 16-17
  torpedoed 18-19
  marries Patricia Matthews 20
  elected Divisional Organiser 22
  confronting the Communists 22-28
  invitation to Ripon Hall 29-31
  Industrial Liaison Officer 32-4
  difficulties with Board of Social Responsibility 35
  the Barrow strike 36-8
  the Pilkington strike 39-45
  crisis at Rolls-Royce 46-8
  Linwood strike 48-9
  ECIM 50-2
  conferences 53
  recollections of Jim Chivers 55
  friendship with Max Baldwin 55-6
  confronting demonic influence 56
  setting up two new unions 59-62
  education 63-6
  first Brussels conference 67-8
  the Paris venture 70-1
  evening years: Cumbria Grand 72-3
  presidents, patrons and trustees 73-6
  journey to Moscow 77-81
  the last months 82-3
Communists xiii-xv
  failure to control Labour movement 6
  battles with Tom 20-8
  infiltration 36
  the Pilkington strike 40
  Spanish trades unions 57, 70
  the Moscow visit 77-8
  failure of Communism 84, 107
  personnel management 94-5
Common Cause 115
Conservative Party 8, 9, 30
Conway, Jim 27

127

Co-operative Movement 8
Corrymeela Community 57
Craven, Sir Charles 12-13
Cumbria Grand 72-3
Daily Express x, 25
Daily Mail ix
Daily Mirror x, 21, 22
ECIM (European Christian Industrial Movement) ix, 50-2, 64, 68-71, 73-6, 82, 99, 107, 116, 117
Feather, Vic 20, 43
Focolare 57, 69
ffrench-Beytagh, Revd Canon Gonville 50
GACAA (Graphic and Creative Art Association) 60
George V xiv
Girlings 48
Gowland, Revd Bill ix, 54, 59, 75
Grundy, Tom 39
Hearsey, Arthur 8-9
Heath, Edward 75
Hitler xiii
Hook, Rt Rev Ross, MC 74
Industrial Committee (Church of England) 29-30, 35, 37, 47, 76, 115
IRIS (Industrial Research and Information Services) 20, 21
Jefferson, Thomas 45
Labour Party xiii-xiv, 6, 8, 9, 20, 26, 46
Leicester, Bishop of 50, 67-9, 73, 76, 114
Lenin xii, 5, 21, 56
MacDonald, Ramsay xiv
Marx, Karl xi
McGrath, Matt 40-1
Millom Town Council 54
NGA (National Graphical Association), 59
North Western *Evening Mail* x, 36
NUGMW (National Union of General and Municipal Workers) 39-40

OECD (Organisation for Economic Co-operation and Development) 70-1
Orwell, George x, 3, 5
Peel, Jack 54, 75-6, 114
Pilkington, Alistair 39
Pilkington, David ix, 41, 53
Pilkington, Lord 42-3
Pudor, Father Marie-Joseph 67, 113
Reader's Digest x, 22
St Vedast Church 50
Scanlon, Hugh (Lord) 36
Scargill (conference centre) xi, 54, 55, 111
Schumacher, Christian 57
Sheet Metalworkers Union 32
Sheffield, Bishop of 30, 31
Shipbuilding and Engineering Workers Union 31
Silverman, Sidney 20
SLADE (Society of Lithographic Artists, Designers and Engravers) 59-60
Snowden, Philip xiv
Stainton ix, 72-3, 76, 77
Stalin xi
Stannard, R.W. (Bishop of Woolwich and Dean of Rochester) 10-11, 20
Star ix, 22
Suenens, Cardinal 69
Taylor, A.J.P. x, 5-6
Temple, William (Archbishop of Canterbury) 29, 46
TGWU (Transport and General Workers Union) 51, 62
Thomas, J.H. 6
Times, The x, 29, 46, 47, 49, 84, 115
TUBE (The Union of Bookmakers' Employees) 61-2
TUC (Trades Union Congress) 20, 61, 75, 94
Union of Dyers, Bleachers and Textile Workers 75
Watson, Revd Basil ix, 65, 74-6
Wilson, Harold (Sir) 48, 75